THE FIRE THIS TIME

THE FIRE THIS TIME

AMERICA'S YEAR OF CRISIS

by

MAX HASTINGS

TAPLINGER PUBLISHING COMPANY
NEW YORK

First Published in the United States in 1969 by
TAPLINGER PUBLISHING CO., INC.
29 East Tenth Street
New York, New York 10003

Library of Congress Catalog Card Number: 73-79856

PRINTED IN THE UNITED STATES OF AMERICA

AUTHOR'S NOTE

Because reporters are always being accused of inaccuracy, I
should start by saying that I am a reporter: in the context
of 1968, that means I was making notes on street corners,
trying to catch words and phrases tossed out in the heat of
the moment, writing stories while the events I was describing
were still taking place. In approaching this book, I have tried
to rethink much that happened to me and much that I wrote
at the time. But if I have misquoted or misrepresented, over-
emphasised or underplayed, then it is because I am a bad
reporter, not through deliberate intent. My apologies to any
Presidential candidates who were still saying they were not
candidates at the time I say they were.

MAX HASTINGS

November 1968

FOR
CLARE, D.M.H. AND A.S-J.

CONTENTS

	Introduction	9
1	The Politics of Uncertainty	13
2	Spring has Sprung	33
3	Another Lost Generation	55
4	A New Kind of Ball Game	83
5	A War About Peace	99
6	The Background: Wasps Still Sting	115
7	A Message from Our Sponsors	137
8	Miami to Chicago	151
9	How to Stop Worrying and Learn to Love Main Street	169
	Select Bibliography	179
	Index	183

INTRODUCTION

Between August, 1967, and the Presidential Election of November, 1968, I spent a little over thirteen months in the United States of America. I think my own personal turning point during that period came when Robert Kennedy was assassinated. When the telephone woke me and a friend said: "Isn't it awful about Kennedy being shot?", it was minutes before I was convinced that it was more than a hoax to get me running to the airport. It seemed only days since I was standing in the hot sun of Atlanta watching Martin Luther King's funeral cortège file past in its thousands. And the night before I had been reading a brilliant pamphlet by Abe Fortas, Chief Justice designate of the Supreme Court, entitled "We Have an Alternative to Violence."

I was not a great admirer of Robert Kennedy—less than ever after covering him on the campaign trail several times. But hearing Negro leaders ask in desperation on the day of his death: "What kind of conspiracy is this to destroy everyone in America who cares about the poor and under-privileged?", one realised that even to prove that there is no link between the great American assassinations would be no answer of any kind to their agony. The question had become not *who* killed King, the Kennedys, Malcolm X, Medgar Evers, but *what* killed them? After Kennedy, if not before, the temptation to cry in answer: "American Society!" became harder than ever to resist.

I don't think it was very easy to maintain a clear sense of perspective in America in 1968; when one is almost constantly covering tragedy and disaster, one inevitably loses whatever sense of detachment it is possible for a reporter to maintain. All that I can attempt to do is recall from the stories I wrote at the time, from notes, from reports and from memory, some of the things that seemed to matter at moments when much of America felt nothing mattered any more. Beyond that, one can try to piece together some kind of picture of how America appears to be facing her problems: not in the White House or in Washington so much as at a popular level, at the level at which housewives have been learning to fire revolvers, and there are still many of those who really believe in the virtues of a pre-emptive war against China.

Although I reported many of the events and personalities described for the London *Evening Standard*, my travels in America were originally made possible by an American foundation, the World Press Institute, which every year finances fifteen foreign journalists to spend a year studying the United States. To the World Press Institute, specifically to Harry Morgan, James Toscano and Arthur McDermott, I owe more than I can say. I hope that they feel their efforts on my behalf were not entirely wasted. Beyond them, I owe another debt to the hundreds of Americans who, be they conservative or liberal, racist or integrationist, rich or poor, more than live up to their claim to be the most hospitable people in the world. Thanks also, perhaps, to American politics: the most fascinating spectator sport in the calendar.

AMERICA 1968

The crises, the tragedies, the problems of 1968 stretched over so many areas of such diversity that it is impossible to consider all of them in great detail. And since I have tried to make this a personal account, I have also largely restricted myself to the events and to the situations that I myself covered. It was never really possible to keep any one separate from others, because so many overlapped and collided with each other that year. Even now, it is difficult to look back.

As the winter of 1967 ended, so much seemed funny that could not be funny now. The war in Vietnam was pursuing its wretched course without apparent benefit to either side, while election year seemed unlikely to offer any classic duels. The President, it was assumed, would take some hard knocks. But like a television wrestling match, it seemed pre-ordained that after the bad falls, he would batter his way to re-nomination and grudging re-election. And so everyone laughed with a gloomy confidence that nothing was changing.

It was funny when William Buckley, the high-priest of conservatism, said solemnly: "I never said Bobby Kennedy was ruthless . . ." One could see the joke in a car sticker which read: "Where are you, Lee Harvey Oswald, now that we really need you?"

There was a detective on South Side, Chicago, with whom I toured the ghetto, and asked what percentage of the groups hanging around on the street corners was armed. He laughed too: "What do you mean, what percentage? The whole damn lot!"

Perhaps most amusing of all was Joe Strickland, a Negro journalist with the Detroit News, whose incisiveness and perception lost nothing by being humorously expressed: "Don't you believe all that crap Negroes here are handing out to the Whites about how sorry they are about what happened last month," he told me, a few weeks after the disastrous riots in Detroit. "When one Negro talks to another round here, he says: 'It was a great fire, man!' What do I think myself?" He winked. "It was a great fire, man!"

The politicans, too, were still finding things to laugh about. Although Vice-President Hubert Humphrey didn't adopt the phrase, "The politics of joy", until long afterwards—and even then, he lived to regret it—he always had a facility for seeing the brightest side of a situation even at the least propitious moment. One autumn afternoon in 1967, at his most affable (if long winded), he was positively gay as he talked about the forthcoming election year:

"All this business about fighting within the Democratic Party is always getting overplayed", he remarked lightly. "Remember what Abraham Lincoln said: 'Democrats are always fighting like cats, but when it's all over and they come out at the end, there just seem to be more cats'." Poor Hubert. Whether winning or losing, he has never been lucky in his public pronouncements. But in fairness to his past, the spirit in which he joked that day seemed almost universal at the time. Former Republican Vice-President Richard Nixon was in much the same mood when he suggested that, in 1968, President Johnson might be under considerable pressure to have Robert Kennedy on the Democratic ticket with him. It seemed highly unlikely that Kennedy even wanted to be Vice-President under Lyndon Johnson. But Nixon shrugged off the question with a laugh: "Does Bobby want to be Vice-President? Of course he does! Every struggling young man wants to be Vice-President!"

This is what was lost in the early months of 1968: the potential for taking America lightly, for seeing and listening without becoming desperately intense, overwrought and angry.

Perhaps the most difficult problem of all, as spring began, was to see what perspectives I, an Englishman looking at the United States, could possibly use in considering the nation.

Does the fact that Americans take the violence of their society for granted make them more reasonable, or less so? To what extent are assassinations and riots, political crises and constant upheavals indicative of some great national malaise? President Johnson appeared on television after Robert Kennedy was shot and said that they are not. The international press, whose reactions to that event were widely reported in America at the time, mostly said that they are. But once again, not everyone agreed. I remember a conversation with the doyen of British correspondents in Washington about the use of machine guns and tanks in the big city riots, which seems to an outsider a case of terrifying over-reaction. The correspondent disagreed. "You've got to learn to accept the facts of life over here, old boy. . . ." *What are the "facts of life" in a society, and what the unacceptable nightmares? In the latter half of 1967 in America, there had seemed no immediate necessity to face these questions. But as the dim spring of 1968 darkened into a black summer, they were thrust upon every American to answer as best as he could.*

Once more, the outsider reviewed and re-reviewed the case for the prosecution. Is it right to shiver when a bank manager in Sioux Falls, South Dakota (population 80,000) tells you that he believes in shipping all American Negroes back to Africa? Or should one merely feel that as long as a man of the calibre of John Lindsay is Mayor of New York, all is not yet lost?

Conversations and personalities like these were never far from the forefront in 1968: diverse, complex, bewildering. And because this was also election year, politics could never be forgotten, even in the midst of riots and upheavals.

If in these pages there is an impression that government was almost a vacuum after Lyndon Johnson announced his impending withdrawal, it is because I found myself looking at America more often on the street corners and on the hustings than in Washington. In 1968, few if any of the initiatives seemed to come from the Administration. Events in far away places dictated the responses. I was looking at the events, not the responses.

There were several moments of high political excitement in the year: when the results of the primary election were announced after the bitter campaigns, when candidates came and went to and from the race—sometimes willingly, often less willingly—and, of course, when the outcome of the conventions and of the election itself were declared.

But of all these moments none even now seems to eclipse the drama that surrounded the events of March—the New Hampshire Primary and President Johnson's announcement of his impending abdication; the first great overturns of 1968. In order that these become a little clearer, the process by which Americans choose their Presidents must first be considered briefly. I didn't understand it properly myself until long after New Hampshire had been fought and won. But the political scientists seem to agree that even in the light of all that followed, New Hampshire marked the most sensational political upheaval in recent American history.

CHAPTER I

THE POLITICS OF UNCERTAINTY

"A former small-college sociology and economics professor, he is learned, eloquent and witty but seemingly little
prepared for the gruelling combat of a half-dozen Presidential primaries."

New York Times Election Handbook
on Senator Eugene McCarthy, March, 1968

IT IS PROBABLY largely because America is so vast, so
fragmented and so diverse that Americans take longer than
anyone else in making up their minds about who is to govern
them. It may also be because of the care with which the men
who drew up the nation's constitution built in such a complex
system of checks and balances between executive, legislative and
judiciary—although since those days American politics have
become immensely more complicated than George Washington
can have dreamed even in his wildest nightmares.

What is certain is that in choosing a President, the American
people sit down at the beginning of every election year for a
circus, a battle, a performance which will fascinate and bewilder
the participants themselves almost as much as the rest of the
world.

Understanding the contest which will be decided in the first
part of election year's November is perhaps the easiest part
of all, because it really concerns only two serious candidates—
a Democrat and a Republican—whatever the varying influence
of any third party candidates who try their luck from time to
time. But the struggle between these two men, whoever they
are, only really begins in the previous July or August after each
party has held its nominating convention at which the delegates
have elected the candidate to represent them.

It is the battle for control of these delegates at the convention
that occupies the nation almost from the year's beginning until
August. In the months between, anyone who thinks he is Presidential material can use any means he sees fit, public or private,

in the search for a delegate majority. Delegates to the national party conventions are chosen in various ways : the majority are selected or elected at local party conventions held in each state. To gain their support, an aspiring Presidential candidate may be able to do much of his work behind the scenes, wheeling and dealing, negotiating and bargaining. American political commentators say that these days the old-style, powerful and more or less corruptible local party bosses cannot do as much as they used to in just delivering blocks of delegates to whoever they chose. Perhaps this is not as true as they would like to think. But one thing is certain : delegates chosen at local conventions like to ride a winner, like to feel that the man they support will become the party's Presidential candidate, and are bound to be influenced by any evidence one hopeful or another can produce to prove that he has vote-getting potential and public popularity.

This turns the emphasis to the other method by which some state parties choose their national convention delegates : they let voters in their state cast ballots for one or other of alternative groups of delegates who offer themselves for election with the promise that, if chosen, they will support one or other given candidate at the convention. The result is the Presidential Primary election, what Theodore White, author of *The Making of The President* books, describes as America's most original contribution to the art of democracy. For the primaries have become much more than a means of electing convention delegates. They offer the best available guide to just which Presidential candidate—hitherto, a more or less unknown quantity—looks capable of winning in November. Most states which hold primaries have a place on the ballot form, beside the lists of all the alternative delegates, on which voters can indicate who they would like to see as their party's candidate. Their selection is binding on no one; it is merely a formalised popularity poll to which great political importance has come to be attached. A further subtlety in some primaries, only worth mentioning because of its significance in 1968, is the write-in vote. If a would-be Presidential candidate is too coy or too cautious to ask for his name to be put on the ballot, he can let it be known that he is interested in what people think of his suitability, and if they feel strongly enough in his favour, they can fill in his name in a blank space on the ballot. It is remarkable how many Americans, in the last twenty-five years, have taken the trouble to do so for one candidate or another.

Why do some states have primaries and others not? It is all part of the regionalisation and diversity of the country, of the varying preferences and beliefs. Primaries have only become really significant in recent years, and for a state like New Hampshire, at the most cynical level, the inrush of politicians and reporters is a very useful source of early-tourist income. Minnesota once instituted a Presidential primary when its ex-Governor seemed to have a good chance of becoming President. But he still lost the primary in his home state : Minnesota hasn't had one since. Other states are even now trying to get Presidential primaries written into their constitutions, perhaps because they seem the most democratic method of selecting delegates, perhaps because they are a good way of increasing national interest in a certain area. There have been suggestions that every state should have a primary, but these are rejected mainly on the grounds that the strain on all concerned of having two national elections in a year would be intolerable.

The important difference between the financing of primaries and of the national election is that until the national party has chosen its candidate, none of the rivals for that role have call on the national party funds. They must raise the money for their primary campaigns themselves. This system clearly favours the rich, who can spend as much money as they want on their campaigns, and do. Hubert Humphrey suffered terribly in his primary campaigns against John F. Kennedy in 1960 because of his lack of finance. Eugene McCarthy was obviously less well placed than Robert Kennedy in 1968 to buy television time, charter aircraft, hire top assistants and put out propaganda. This again has produced some pressure for elections to be financed from tax money either at the national or local level. But the pressures and complications seem likely to defeat any measures to this effect in the forseeable future, and the party faithful around the country will continue to be tapped for financial assistance twice every election year—once by the rivals for the nominations, once again by the party and its official candidate once he has been chosen.

There is, however, far more to the primaries than just the colour provided by having not one, but dozens of elections succeeding each other during an election year in a sequence developed by chance more than planning. The total number of delegates a candidate can amass even by winning every single primary is insufficient to gain the nomination of his party. But it is a great help in winning over delegates from non-primary states who will often waver to see which way the wind is blowing. Generally, behind-the-scenes negotiating for delegates is the privilege of a candidate who is either a member of the innermost party establishment, or very close to that establishment. Fighting one's way to the nomination by entering primaries, showing wide popularity, and making it embarrassing for a convention *not* to nominate you is the rough, the exhausting and the most embarrassing way of seeking victory. But it is often the only route open to a Eugene McCarthy or a Robert Kennedy—the outsiders. New Hampshire, Wisconsin, Indiana, Oregon, Nebraska, West Virginia, California—these are some of the states which hold primary elections whose importance varies from election year to election year. In 1968, political shocks followed each other in rapid succession partly because so many of the rules I have outlined above were suddenly and rudely broken. But the theory holds true and it was against this background that the political dramas of the year were played out. Perhaps one can do no more than turn once again to Theodore White, who has done as much as anyone to make American Presidential politics understandable for those of us who started grappling in the dark: "In theory, a primary fight removes the nomination of candidates from the hands of the cynical party leadership and puts it directly in the hands of the people who make the party. When indeed theory matches fact (for in some states, primaries are absurdly meaningless), primary contests result in disastrous and unforgettable explosions. A genuine primary is a fight within the family of the party and, like any family fight, is apt to be more bitter and leave more enduring wounds than battle with the November enemy. In primaries, ambitions spurt from nowhere; unknown men carve their mark; old men are sent relentlessly to their political graves; bosses and leaders may be humiliated or unseated. . . ."

White wrote those words in 1960. Nothing that happened in the election campaign of 1968 could make him want to change a line.

And yet, one remembers March . . .

March, when bothering about the primaries seemed so "ab-

surdly meaningless", when we were all so certain that Lyndon
Johnson would be coming back. I met only one man in the days
before March 31st who was certain that Lyndon Johnson had
decided not to run again : J. Edward Day, John F. Kennedy's
former Postmaster-General. At the time, he seemed to be standing very much on a limb with his assured predictions. During
John F. Kennedy's election campaign in 1960, observers had
been able to write that he had "chosen the primary route" to
the Democratic nomination, as opposed to Lyndon Johnson's
backstage negotiating, that he had chosen to try to prove his
overwhelming public support as a means of convincing the party
convention that he was the man who could win the national
election for the party. But Kennedy had not been fighting an
incumbent President. And the Washington press, all 1968's
spring, had been eager to point out how many countless years
it was since a party convention had refused to re-nominate an
incumbent President. Johnson was only entered for primaries
in those states which automatically put all Democratic and
Republican Presidential prospects on their ballots without con-
sulting them. In other states, however, the Democratic establish-
ments were running write-in campaigns for the President,
because nothing is nicer than a vote of confidence that is apparently unsought. In every state, Democrats were expected to
write-in Lyndon Johnson's name in overwhelming numbers.

Among the Republicans, it seemed that the only man presenting an active challenge to Richard Nixon's strongly-running
round-up of primary votes and convention delegates was
Governor George Romney of Michigan, who had been out since
early in the year campaigning in New Hampshire, site of the
first of the year's primaries on March 12th. Governor Nelson
Rockefeller of New York, whose name had been on everyone's
lips as a liberal Republican hopeful, now seemed so passive in
his attitude to the whole race that the press discussed Romney's
chances of beating Nixon with keen interest—if only because
any competition seems better than no competition at all.

But Romney had lost many months before when he used one
ill-guarded phrase in public : he said he had been "brain-
washed" by the army in Vietnam into believing that the war
could be won militarily. Americans don't want Presidents who
are so easily misled. And Romney never seemed to have the
force, the hardness of a potential Chief Executive. He is a

Mormon, and despite all his protestations of liberalism, the fact that his creed is ambiguously illiberal on the subject of race relations had already made him suspect in many eyes. He always seemed an amiable figure, although increasingly at a loss for words : a disastrous failing in a campaigner. But when, only a few short weeks before polling day, Romney suddenly announced his withdrawal from the race, America seemed surprised, but unconscious of any great sense of loss. Romney had withdrawn because his opinion pollsters confirmed popular suspicion : nobody wanted him.

Thus once again, every eye was focused on the Democrats. Richard Nixon, unopposed, was of little interest in the New Hampshire primary, and already seemed to have an excellent chance of securing his party's nomination. Who was left? Lyndon Johnson.

.The President . . .

When I arrived in America months before, it seemed almost impossible that the nation could find new words of scorn for him. Theodore White said he felt tempted to call 1968 "The Making of a Tragedy". Never, he said sadly, had such vital issues been debated by such disappointing candidates.

Lyndon Johnson, it appeared, was the victim of more personal hatred than any American President in recent memory. Indeed, it became a hot debating point whether he was more cordially disliked than Roosevelt in 1940, or Truman at the time of Korea, with a majority agreeing that Johnson had eclipsed them in unpopularity.

Perhaps it all had something to do with what Murray Kempton was talking about months later when he said that one could never be light-hearted about a major national politician again, that whatever one's feelings about a man, one would always respect the fact that he is there, that he is taking risks and making decisions in a way that could never be truly funny again. Could one laugh now at students burning Lyndon Johnson in effigy, or saying the sort of things people were saying that spring?

"Don't spit in the soup. We've all got to eat" was a supposed Johnsonism from one of the best-sellers of the time, *Quotations from Chairman LBJ*. The fact that it sold so well could be said to reflect most accurately how so many of us, Americans and foreigners, wanted to think of Lyndon Johnson—as the Texan ranch hand, more at home at a barbecue than a state dinner, who would use an electric cattle prod on Congress if he could. By March, criticism of the President often seemed to have been reduced to pure malice.

I was with a group of foreign correspondents who met Lyndon Johnson towards the end of March. He is a disconcerting man to talk to face to face : he has a way of looking you straight in the eye that makes it very hard to look him back. In forty minutes, he came very close to making some of us feel almost guilty that we opposed the war. Leaning across the table to each man in turn, gesticulating forcefully as he made his points, he talked about knowing what it is to be young, and understanding what makes young people dissent. He looks powerful, the sort of factory foreman one would hate to argue with or, more appropriately, the kind of army non-commissioned officer who scares the daylights out of recruits on the drill field.

After that meeting, one could not retain any doubts about his complete sincerity and conviction in the justice of his Vietnam policies. But he ended it by making a bad mistake : having stood up, said goodbye, and walked out of the room, he suddenly swung round and came back in. Still with a fixed half-smile on his face, he said, "I'd like to ask you all one question—have any of you changed your minds about any of the things you'd read and heard now that you've been here?" There was just an embarrassed silence. It seemed desperately depressing that a President, of all people, should admit that he either wanted or needed the answer to a question like that. In a couple of sentences, he had slipped from his pedestal. He was once again in the position of a politician pursuing unpopular policies who wants very much to believe that his critics are motivated by lack of understanding rather than deliberate opposition.

And yet in the days before New Hampshire, who or what could possibly stand between the President and an ultimately successful election year?

Only one man marred Johnson's immediate political view : Minnesota Senator Eugene McCarthy. The previous autumn, McCarthy had announced that he felt so strongly about the errors of the Administration's Vietnam policy that he proposed to challenge Johnson in some of election year primary campaigns. New Hampshire was the first of the season, so in New Hampshire in the spring Eugene duly presented himself. To a press corps starved of news, within a few weeks salvation presented itself. Around McCarthy gathered the most incredible army American politics had ever seen. From the length and breadth of the whole East Coast came the nation's young, with their sleeping bags and their jeans and dreams of the apparently impossible, to hoist into the saddle their white knight against the President. "The Children's Crusade", it became called. McCarthy, the press felt, would be lucky to get ten per cent of the Democratic vote on polling day. His obvious dislike of the whole business of campaigning, his low-key style, his virtual political obscurity at a national level—all this put him, if not beyond the pale, at least crawling on its fringes. Nevertheless, his youthful army was gaining him the publicity he desperately needed, but disdained to seek for its own sake. It added the touch of spectator sport to an election that seemed to need it very badly.

During the last months of 1967 and the first of the new year, Lyndon Johnson must have become acutely aware of how closely he himself had come to be linked with the "credibility gap" in so many American minds. For it had become so much more than a reflection of popular misgiving about the Vietnam war. It expressed a lack of confidence not only in the President's policies but, more important, in his personal integrity and sincerity. This was where McCarthy's student campaigners in New Hampshire found their passionate enthusiasm for his cause : they believed Johnson was not merely wrong, but evil. It's very easy to say that the young can always be stirred up to fight for a cause, and in many ways this is true. But it had not been true in American national politics. The student activists in post-war America had done their protesting outside the political framework. Thus the shock was to be all the greater when it was seen what they could achieve working within the system. On polling day in New Hampshire, it wasn't really surprising that the American press, dealing with a phenomenon outside their experience, still had no real idea of what was going on around them.

At March's beginning, McCarthy still appeared a mere divertissement along the road, a sideshow to brighten up a dull election year. On the wall of one of the McCarthy campaign headquarters in Concord, New Hampshire, was the front page of an old 1952 newspaper, with a headline proclaiming

"KEFAUVER MAKES IT". It was, for the "McCarthy Kids", a reminder that the impossible could be possible, a precedent from the year when Estes Kefauver defeated incumbent President Harry Truman in the upturn of the year. No one attached much significance to it except Eugene's faithful. And even they didn't seem to notice that Kefauver had not gone on to win the nomination, or that Harry Truman had subsequently decided not to run for re-election.

Eugene McCarthy was a one-issue candidate, he said so himself. He was fighting a campaign with a hopelessly unprofessional team—the only expert was former John F. Kennedy adviser Richard Goodwin, who was reported to be continually frustrated by the slap-happy approach of his colleagues. And most of all, although very many Americans obviously felt unhappy about the Vietnam war, the idea of their voting for a man who was saying (more or less, he often hedged one way or the other) "peace at any price" seemed almost incredible.

For travelling around America that spring, one found in almost every small town or community that someone had a relation or a friend in Vietnam. Beyond that, more and more of them knew someone who had died or been wounded there. Again and again any debate on the war would come back to the same point: "Yes, we should get out. But how can we? We can't just leave it all to the Communists, we can't have seen all those young men killed for nothing. . . ." Loss of face in withdrawal seemed so much more hurtful than loss of Vietnam itself. The myth of a nation never defeated in a war seemed desperately worth preserving. It is often frightening to discover just how many Americans there are who still regard Communism with the old-style paranoiac terror. But there is an even larger body who are neither vicious nor violent, merely quietly determined, uncomplicated people who live their lives according to a very deep belief in what they think America stands for. This belief has become increasingly embarrassing to a government in Washington seeking solutions to the nation's domestic problems which conflict with frontier principles.

But in the matter of Vietnam, it seemed that Administration policy and small-town credo were in agreement: "Yes, war is terrible but we have a duty. . . ." There are many places in America where they will remind you, sometimes quietly, occasionally viciously, that if John F. Kennedy had lived to run for a second term, he was very far from certain of re-election. And many, many Americans still have a strong feeling of conscious pride that they saved Europe in two World Wars. This again is a theme which is quickly taken up in any debate between an Englishman and an American on Vietnam.

The manner in which the outpost of Khe Sanh was assuming almost the significance of a Verdun to the American army— *"ils ne passeront pas"*—with all its attendant fears and obstinacies; the talk of George Wallace and his third party preventing either side gaining a clear majority in the election and causing it to be thrown into the House of Representatives for a result achieved by bargaining; the strong threat of riots in the cities during the summer ... there was so much else to be afraid of on March 12th, that to be in New Hampshire seemed like an educational holiday.

It is one of the smallest of the fifty states and also, as part of green New England, one of the prettiest. Not that there was much green to be seen : the week before the election, snow came and went, covered everything and then partly melted again, leaving a huge sludgy mess. Through that sludge for weeks now had trudged McCarthy, occasionally Richard Nixon—the latter running an apparently almost irrelevant errand canvassing for support against no opposition—but never Lyndon Johnson. Fighting primaries against belligerent senators hardly seemed part of the business of governing the greatest nation on earth. But the Johnson write-in campaign had been run under the overall direction of the state's Democratic Governor, who had informed the electorate a few days before polling day, that a vote for Eugene McCarthy amounted to a vote for Hanoi. On reflection, the pundits agreed that this was a mistake, that it annoyed far more voters than it won over. But still, how could the Senator beat odds of this kind? Again and again the question was asked, with just a slight change of tone perceptible now : was it possible that perhaps he could by some miracle dent the President? In fairness to the American press, one must admit that by election day there was more than just a hint of surprises in the air.

March 12th, election night, in the hours before the polls finally closed, the whole election colony began to congregate round the McCarthy headquarters. With the unofficial Johnson headquarters in an unprepossessing flat in the state's biggest city,

Manchester, and Richard Nixon in New York leaving his base in a large and ugly hotel in Concord almost deserted, there seemed nowhere else to be. McCarthy had established himself in a sprawling, modern but very attractive motel a few miles outside Manchester, just off the main state highway. It was a gay place, with a restaurant not as bad as some American steak-houses, and a bar where there was always a row going on because state law insisted that everyone drink sitting down and all the out-of-state journalists and party workers persisted in trying to stand up.

The three television networks had commandeered their usual huge acreage for studio space and camera platforms, and everybody who knew anybody with a room in the hotel kept trying to cajole them into turning it into a communal office. One big room had been established as the results receiving centre, and it was there as evening came, that party workers, the newsmen, the TV cameras and the casual spectators gathered into a crowd that made movement hazardous and ordinary conversation impossible. It was hot, because of the television lights and the low ceiling. And it was exciting because, of all those watching the election, the "McCarthy Kids" there that night were absolutely sure that "Gene" was going to bring home a vote that would startle America.

Around that room between eight in the evening and two the next morning, a party began which was to go on for many weeks to come. What does one ever remember about parties? That everybody was so happy they wanted to cry, that they all got drunk without having had a drink, that when Eugene himself finally appeared to say his quiet words of thanks, there was an emotion there which completely outstripped politics or elections?

They hoisted their victory banner over the results board because exact numbers of votes didn't matter, their man had come so close to the President as to set fire to his coat tails. Forty-two per cent to the President's forty-nine per cent, and the kids were talking about it as they lay on the floors in the corridors because there was nowhere else to go. McCarthy, with the style that made them love him, had said that morning that he would be making no further comments on the election until the concession statement came through from the White House. To the kids, the concession statement was in the figures.

Someone laughed and said that if Lyndon Johnson was in the habit of executing bearers of bad tidings, the White House would be heaped up with corpses by the morning. Everybody had a wonderful five minutes conjuring up visions of the scene in Washington as the President read the results. It wasn't just a near-as-no-matter victory in an election, it seemed to be evidence that democracy not only still worked, but could be seen to work. It was the triumph of the individual over the machine, of conscience over political calculation. Come to that, it seemed a victory for good over evil, of peace over war. It was all so easy, that night—no complications, no dilemmas, no moral divides—the answers were all there in the faces of the students who had hoisted Eugene into the driving seat. Nobody cared about Richard Nixon being given a few minutes of television time to say thank you to the Republicans who had voted for him against no opposition. There is a great hit song from the musical, *Man of La Mancha*, called "The Impossible Dream" and somebody suggested making it McCarthy's theme. It sounded like a wonderful idea. People were asking how they could get to Wisconsin to take their sleeping-bags there and start all over again for the April 2nd primary. That sounded like a wonderful idea too. The snow had been falling hard for much of the evening and everything outside was wonderfully white, with a couple of girls running round and round making patterns in the snow in their glee: VICTORY...

Any serious political commentator must accuse me of getting things out of perspective, when I look back on New Hampshire now, perhaps because I'm young myself, I was carried away by the impact of it all more than most. Now, to remember that night seems like recalling the years before the First World War, like a honeymoon that one only knew was a honeymoon after it ended. New Hampshire was the beginning of something— or the end of something. It was the one great evening of 1968 on which feelings could be wholly, entirely and utterly unclouded, when everything was happening and everything seemed right.

It was the evening that made one wake up. In all the months I had been in America before March 12th, I had seen many places, many people, and heard a great deal said. But somehow it had not provoked one to feel anything, not aroused the fascination that one needs to learn anything at all. That night, I could not help being provoked. John Kennedy, talking of White's

The Making of the President, is said to have remarked that it was a great book except that it made all its characters seem so much larger than life. This was the night of 1968 when I found people and the ideas becoming larger than life. Later in the McCarthy campaign, a poster appeared showing him surrounded by laughing students with the caption, "OUR CHILDREN HAVE COME HOME". The caption did not lie. The lazy Senator from Minnesota had done something for America that most Americans still do not properly appreciate.

*   *   *

A staff writer of the *Washington Post* began his report from Milwaukee on Saturday March 30th, a mere fortnight after New Hampshire: "It is five days before the Wisconsin Democratic primary, which presumably will have something to do with the election of a President..." He was proving, for the second but far from the last time of the year, that sarcastically taking the obvious for granted was a very dangerous thing to do.

Why did Wisconsin sound so much less interesting than New Hampshire, when it should have been more so, with McCarthy having a real chance of winning a numerical victory? Was it because when those first days of euphoria after March 12th wore off, America realised that the President's prestige had taken a bad blow but that his election chances had changed little if at all? So few people around America knew McCarthy's name—indeed, it was claimed that some of those who voted for him in New Hampshire were convinced that they were backing a Vietnam hawk. And it had always been said that New Hampshire was a freak state where anything could happen. Now, in Wisconsin, McCarthy would be fighting on the most advantageous ground, in his home area of the Mid-West, in a state where his organisation was excellent. The President, it seemed, was taking Wisconsin seriously. He had dispatched several members of his cabinet to campaign for him there, with mediocre results. The press, conscious of having so grossly underestimated McCarthy in New Hampshire, were now giving him prima donna coverage. The opinion polls showed that his omens were favourable. It simply seemed that victory in Wisconsin or no, Eugene McCarthy could never persuade a Democratic convention to nominate him, if only because his very existence as a campaigner was a contemptuous slap in the face for the party establishment.

And there was one other thing too, by that Sunday, March 31st: Robert Francis Kennedy had declared himself as a Presidential candidate.

Kennedy's entrance into the race had reduced many of the students who were fighting so hard for McCarthy, not to mention a large slice of the American electorate, to total fury. By joining the battle within days of New Hampshire, having refused to mount his own attack on Johnson or even to help McCarthy, despite his own declared opposition to the President's policies, Kennedy had at a stroke resurrected every doubt that had ever been cast on his integrity. I remember a Kennedy aide remarking bitterly: "If Bobby helps an old lady across the road, people ask why he's done it." It was difficult to understand the man's surprise. To all those who did not know Kennedy and could judge him only on his public performance, this was the final straw, the ultimate act of calculating ruthlessness, cashing in on the rewards of another man's superior courage and far greater gamble.

More than that, however, it seemed an overwhelming gamble against poor odds. With Kennedy in, it was taken for granted that poor under-organised, under-financed and under-publicised Eugene McCarthy would be rapidly trampled underfoot in the primaries to come, even if he refused to make terms with Robert F. Kennedy. But Kennedy's disadvantages in a straight battle with the President seemed almost as great as McCarthy's. He would be fighting all the patronage and political influence that came to Lyndon Johnson from possession of his office; he would be under the disadvantage of entering the race with none of the years or even months of preparation that had been available to his late brother in 1960; and he would be struggling against the tag of ruthlessness and opportunism which some said, wrongly as it was to appear, would alienate the young on whom the Kennedys had traditionally relied for much support. Kennedy was running all right, and running very fast—massing research material, convention delegate files and helpers, in days to his brother's months. And in a strange way it was very moving to see the gathering of the old clan around him to prepare for the battle: Stephen Smith, Theodore Sorensen, Arthur

Schlesinger, Pierre Salinger—the old men of the New Frontier for whom so much that had ended in November, 1963, now seemed to be revived. It didn't matter whether you loved Kennedy or hated him, one had to be fascinated by the manner in which he went to war, with the press once again talking of the "Irish Mafiosi", campaign headquarters rushed into being in Washington's rather dilapidated Dodge House Hotel, and love, hate, but most of all, action, swirling everywhere he went.

The strange thing about that March Sunday was that in a strange innocence, one felt that political normalcy had returned. The shocks had gone as far as they could go. One read the Sunday papers to catch up on what Stokeley Carmichael had been doing and Congress hadn't (it was almost impossible to take the 90th Congress wholly seriously), on who was currently suspected of robbing the till, and who had just declared that he was definitely not a Presidential candidate. The announcement of the President's 9 p.m. television appearance seemed more of an afterthought than a news item. The Open Housing Bill was still driftwood on the sleepy beach of Congress, the economic debate seemed to have become more intense but further than ever from a solution, and Eugene McCarthy rated a column or two in most papers for his activities in Wisconsin. Hubert Humphrey was on an official visit to Mexico, his vast brow apparently unsullied by any inner worries or knowledge. And we all laughed at the recall of a television joke of the kind everyone in America has to try to laugh at these days—a satire on newscasts of the future, which suggested one item of Stokeley Carmichael in 1998 as Governor of Alabama, welcoming the first white student to be admitted to the state university in twenty years.

Bored, we were trying a little bookmaking on the probable course of the President's television speech. Ten to one against his announcing a cessation of the bombing of Vietnam; six to one that he will announce a further troop escalation; odds on that he will remind the American people of the need to stand firm and united at this difficult time . . .

Whatever he planned to say, no one was expecting very much sparkle in the way he said it. It is well known that Johnson doesn't like television appearances, simply because he doesn't come over well. His attempts to grapple with the electronic medium have merely served to reinforce the country barbecue image. On the screen, he usually looks fleshy, unhealthy and sloppily dressed (it is a surprise on meeting him to find that he not only looks tanned and healthy, but also neatly well dressed). His televised press conferences were few and far between, even after one highly successful performance in the autumn of 1967 when he departed from practice and ranged around the room using a cord microphone, moving to his questioners and looking much more impressive than when tied to a rostrum, which makes him uneasy. His formal speeches on national policy prior to March 31st had merely provided more ammunition for his mimics.

Thus no one was surprised, that Sunday night, that he appeared on the screen looking little different from the Lyndon Johnson of old. He was blowing hot and cold again, mesmerising viewers and newsmen with the words "stopping the bombing", then causing a great "Aaah" of disappointment and cynicism when it became clear that he meant only *partially* stopping the bombing. He mentioned an increase in the troop commitment in Vietnam in almost the same breath as talking of "a substantial de-escalation". Somebody watching with me sighed and said : "He's the only man in America who would have the nerve to talk about major de-escalation while making a major escalation". By 9.30 p.m. interest had cooled. It was, it seemed, the mixture as before.

So I was reaching over to switch off the set when he seemed to be starting an appeal to place Vietnam above the level of mere politics. Then we thought we heard him say : "I shall not seek . . . will not accept . . ." and no one quite believes it is true. After all that has gone before, you can only slump back in the chair and close your eyes : America in 1968 was full of so many complexities of race, social problems, domestic unrest and worry about war abroad. Now, suddenly, the nation has acquired a new dimension. Election year has come alive in the most staggering fashion.

The announcer is back. He is saying that the President's statement was a shock to even the studio staff. He adds, for the first time that week—not for the last this year : "The following programmes are being cancelled . . ."

It is hardly surprising that on April Fool's Day, 1968, when I was flying in Robert Kennedy's campaign plane to Philadelphia to watch the shell-shocked Presidential candidate deliver some of the worst speeches he ever made, no one in America could recognise a lull in the crises for what it was. By Thursday, Art Buchwald was shaking his head and trying to imagine a world without LBJ: "I'm against them all, but he was best to be against. Who can I hate now?" Richard Nixon had begun his self-imposed moratorium on discussion of Vietnam until the results of the President's peace offensive were known. And Hubert Humphrey had returned from Mexico trying to look as if, of course, he'd known about everything all along—perhaps he had, but . . .

I remember the student working for Kennedy who stood beside the news tape shaking his head as another story about the President's withdrawal came across, saying: "Why, why, why? He had all the marbles in his pocket and now he's just thrown them to Bobby . . ." Democrats on Capitol Hill were talking of a "Draft Johnson" movement, and there were those who were saying the President had planned it all along as part of his triumphal re-election scheme. But Pierre Salinger, the former White House press secretary working with Kennedy, was looking more than ever like the cat about to get the cream in a jumbo-sized carton.

Kennedy himself was starting a mammoth nation-wide campaign tour (although his campaign plan called for overwhelming emphasis on the handful of states which hold key primary elections). Rather ominously for his prospects, it seemed, Lyndon Johnson's withdrawal had brought few of the nation's major Democratic power figures into the Kennedy camp. Hubert Humphrey still wasn't saying whether he planned to enter the Presidential race. Senator Eugene McCarthy's win in Tuesday's Wisconsin primary election had made little of its expected impact. There were some half-hearted attempts at analysing its significance—whether the Johnson "sympathy" vote had been larger or smaller than expected, whether the turn-out for Richard Nixon could be called a victory . . . but nobody really felt much interest. Both Democrat and Republican had been fighting against shadowy opposition, with the President out of the running and no other major Republican's name on the party ballot. Real interest among the Democrats had already begun to centre on Indiana, where on May 7th Kennedy and McCarthy would face each other head-on for the first time (although even there, the battle was somewhat confused by the presence of a popular state Governor running as a "favourite son" candidate).

Then on Thursday night, in the length of time it takes for a rifle bullet to travel 204 feet, politics and politicians totally receded from the national consciousness. Martin Luther King was a man from America's South, and Memphis is a Southern city. But in the weekend that followed the assassination, it was neither Southerners nor white men who died to expiate the crime. It was almost entirely Negroes in the ghettoes of the North, in more than a hundred cities across the country. I came from Memphis to Chicago amidst reports of "uncontrollable" looting and wholesale destruction. The reports did not lie. On Chicago's West Side, early that Saturday morning, the urban racial crisis had once again exploded into vicious torment.

CHAPTER 2

SPRING HAS SPRUNG

"Don't attach any special significance to the fact that our
targets are black ..."

Federal Bureau of Investigation
firearms instructor, October, 1967

I ᵻHAVE NEVER SEEN a war. That is to say, walking
down West Side, Chicago, on Saturday, April 6th, 1968, a few
hours before dawn, I had never before seen wanton destruction,
only once (and that not in America) seen police and troops
carrying loaded weapons for the express purpose of shooting
at live targets. Most of all, I had never seen large numbers of
human beings very scared. My generation has been reared on
war books and war films, war memoirs and war museums.
Surely this should mean that one knows war when one sees it. It
was all there that Saturday—the flames, the troops, the misery,
the chaos. But how can one accept such a spectacle as real, when
to reach it I'd merely strolled out of the calm of a luxury hotel
and ordered a taxi to take me there as if I was going to the
cinema?

Like any war, it was no game to those who were fighting it.
But to an outsider uninvolved in the battle, it was almost embarrassing to feel afraid. I couldn't get a taxi driver to take
me all the way into the area and I had to pay double fare to
be dropped off at the closest exit from one of the city motorways.
After that, the game stopped for the length of some ten blocks
of buildings, which was the distance I ran before I reached the
police lines. When I left the taxi, I was very unnerved to find
myself alone : I had expected to find every street overrun with
police and troops. Instead, I had to start walking through the
streets.

First one just passed piles of debris. Then there were the
wrecked cars, then the wrecked shops and finally the shops that
were still being looted. There was a furniture store above which

hung a sign proclaiming gaily, "Spring has sprung", with a handful of dim figures rapidly picking over the pathetic wreckage for anything that might have been overlooked by the first wave of pillagers. There were occasional black faces crossing the street, sometimes running, sometimes strolling casually and indifferently. Two crossed towards me, and I started running because, although they made no hostile movement, I was a white face, the only one in sight, and theirs were black. It didn't matter what one felt about race that night, one could only fear black. Because I had read the accounts of previous city riots in America, I was acutely conscious of every window I passed : I felt the easiest target in the world for any sniper within range. One forgot the Riot Report published the previous month, which concluded that almost every riot death had been the result not of Negro but police or military fire. It seemed incredible that everything was so completely silent, until one realised that when not a car is moving any city is quiet. The silence was broken only by the futile clanging of endless burglar alarms. They rang on and on, hour after hour on West Side that night, with no one to switch them off, as they trembled above shattered shopfronts.

It was very easy to know which way to go because, as the sky began to lighten, I could see only a few hundred yards away a huge pillar of smoke hanging above the city. There were others, large and small, behind me on the other side of the motorway.

Then suddenly, I was on Roosevelt Street, centre of the destruction, stopping to pause for breath beside the comforting bulk of a police patrol car, from the windows of which protruded two shotguns. Once again, any semblance of reality ended : I knew I was only watching yet another of those endless films about the London blitz. Walking up that street, jumping huge pools of water from the fire hoses, standing aside as truckloads of troops roared past and making detours around clusters of tired and dirty firemen who still laboured on, I felt like a trespasser, like a spectator on a film set who has accidentally walked in front of the camera. Police cars parked everywhere, their occupants heavily armed; sullen groups of Negro men watching indifferently as Whitey sweats to save their shops and homes; a Negro running frantically around the corner trying to dodge two patrolmen who effortlessly seize him, grab him in an arm lock and whistle for a car to take him away. Who knows what he's done? This sort of night, nobody much cares.

Walking, walking, walking up the street and as far as the eye can see on either side, there is just fire and wreckage. Some buildings blaze furiously, others merely smoulder amidst an occasional crash of falling wreckage. Those which are not burnt or burning are just smashed, their contents lying scattered, their interiors broken ruins. I saw two women, one young and one middle-aged, clamber out of a refuge to see the dawn. They found little to say. They just stood and gazed, aghast.

The police were calm. They sat in their cars, talked, chewed gum and said they figured the worst was about over. They weren't worried about the looters roaming the streets. Hours before, they had faced the decision as to whether it was justifiable to turn a shotgun on a teenager "running up the street with a couple of sports coats in his hand". They had decided it was not. It was to be left to Chicago's Mayor, Richard Daley, to tell them later that they had disgraced his city by their restraint.

The National Guard* were something else again. Standing up in their trucks as they moved through the streets, they had their guns pointed outwards. There were many fingers curled around the triggers, and very many scared faces. A police-car driver suggested I go down to the precinct station where operations were being controlled. I had only walked a few yards when two Guardsmen stopped me with pointed bayonets. I showed them a press card and told them I was heading for

* My experiences with the National Guard varied considerably on the several occasions I had contact with them during my time in America. In Chicago during the April riots, they were alarmingly lacking in confidence. Even as an unarmed correspondent, I felt far less worried about the problems of specific situations than most of the Guardsmen appeared to be, notably one jeepload I rode with, who loaded their rifles while still in downtown Chicago.

But at the Democratic Convention in August, the Guard were displaying a far more reasonable attitude to the confrontation than the Chicago police. Several Guardsmen took trouble to explain to journalists how much they regretted the nature of this job, and I never saw a Guardsman indulge in the kind of wanton sadism so common among the police.

The British Territorials derive far more confidence from their high percentage of Regular and ex-Regular NCOs, and the quality of volunteers for part-time service is notably higher. To an outside observer, the Guard's greatest weakness seems to stem from the Other Ranks' well-justified contempt for their own NCOs and officers.

the police station. They were unimpressed and called their officer, a major. He was about 5 feet 4 inches in height, wearing a helmet low over his eyes, and a revolver in an open holster. He was quite hysterical.

After firing off a five-minute string of quite inexplicable obscenity, he sent me "under arrest" to the police station accompanied by two of his men who, he told me, were under instructions to grab me at once "if you start making a move they don't like . . ." It's not easy to protest when the army is in control, so a ludicrous scene was played out with the two soldiers following me down the street with rifles up. "Don't walk so fast, mac, this isn't a race . . ."

At the police station, the desk officer was unsurprised, "The Guard? Aw hell, they've been behaving like a bunch of jittery kids all night," he remarked with some disgust. The police were tired, but making a lot of cracks. They had just cornered four alleged snipers. "How did we persuade them to come out? Call it mutual agreement. We just asked nicely!" Everybody laughed.

Officers were still moving in and out with suspects accused of looting or sniping. An old Negro man came in to ask if his son had been seen. Later came a woman on the same mission. This was war, their children's absence from home could mean that they were either dead, captured or merely fleeing from the occupation forces. I came out of the police station with a young cop who was reloading his revolver. "I only fired once in the air to stop somebody," he explained. "Will I be out again tonight? Everybody's going to be out again tonight."

That Saturday night, however, West Side was quiet. That is to say, of course, quiet by the standards of the hour: scattered shots, firebombings, unnaturally silent streets saturated with armed lawmen—an uneasy peace.

But the message had not reached the National Guard. They were moving out of their armoury in downtown Chicago with the air of men going out to battle. The soldiers in the jeep in which I rode stopped briefly as soon as we left headquarters to load their weapons, although still several miles from the danger zone. Perhaps they had been infected by the nervousness of the city's newspapers, which had been running headlines all day that suggested the disorders were still in full rampage. Later that night I remember talking to a disgruntled picture editor at one office, irate because he had had a photographer standing by all night to go out to the first big fire to find a colour picture for next day's front page. There had been no big fires, he sighed. In the centre of West Side, still nervous Guardsmen seemed amazed that one was walking the streets, although with police and troops everywhere violence seemed almost impossible.

All that was to be seen that night were the groups of Negro youths wandering the streets then as after every riot, jeering at the alertness and urgency of Whitey's movements. A psychiatrist from the City Board of Health who was walking with me remarked: "Isn't it pathetic to see them in their impotence? They show it by their actions, when rioting and burning is the most extreme display of impotence. And yet, although they know it themselves, they've still got all of us frightened to hell . . ."

*   *   *

It seems very odd now, that the 1965 riot in the Watts section of Los Angeles can be mentioned as a mere afterthought when one talks of "Detroit, Newark, Washington, Chicago, and, oh yes, Watts". For while at the time that it happened, Watts shocked America, it seemed almost an irrelevance when attention on the country's racial problems was still focused almost exclusively on the South.

Detroit and Newark, of course, changed all that. When one talks of the Negro in America, of the crisis facing the nation, one is assumed to be referring to the tragedies of the Northern cities, of the danger of the simmering ghettoes. That in itself is an indication that the Northern riots did what every Northern white prefers to believe that they did not—stir the country into some kind of movement, however sluggish. The tragedies and frustrations of the Negro in the South were set aside and almost forgotten by most white Americans. Mississippi is several hundred miles away and its inhabitants seem insufficiently aware of their own existences to present a threat of rampage and destruction.

But in Chicago, in Detroit, in Philadelphia, in every Northern city from coast to coast, the bank clerk living in his suburban villa can understand very clearly a message of possible disaster to his home, his life and his security. How he feels about it, once he has understood it, depends on many things. Very often, he merely calls for more police, approves a higher city budget to allow them to be provided with armoured cars and lets his wife learn to fire a revolver. Sometimes, he will face a mental battle between fear and his faith in the American Dream. Fear dictates that the Negro be rehoused, found jobs, given welfare benefits. But the American Dream despises charity and rejects the idea of giving anything to those who have not won it for themselves.

It's amazing how powerful that Dream remains throughout America. In city after city across the country, I have heard every kind of American say that he accepts the need to do "anything to stop any more of these damn riots". But pay higher taxes? Make America the land of the free hand-out, —worst of all, of the socialist state? There is deep resistance to the idea of "rewarding" the rioters. There is a constant plea for time. "Sure, something has got to be done. But rioting isn't going to get them anywhere, and if they riot, I say use any means necessary to maintain order. Would you let a mob come runnin' in and burn your home and then tell you afterwards that it was a social protest?" These were some of the people who voted for Richard Nixon and George Wallace in 1968.

Psychologists and urbanologists deduced very quickly after the riots of 1967 that it is far more frustrating to live in the ghetto of a great American city, surrounded on every side by the wanton wealth of the richest society on earth, than to be eking out an even more desperate existence in the Mississippi Delta, where most of the population are scarcely aware that anything better exists.

The simple statistics of life in the urban ghetto are perhaps the most frightening testament to the scale of America's domestic crisis. The Moynihan Report* issued in March, 1965, indicated that nearly one quarter of all urban Negro marriages are dissolved; that 3.8 million American Negroes live in families headed by women; that in New York City, fathers are for some reason absent in 30.2 per cent of all Negro families; and that at least one quarter of all Negro children born in the cities are illegitimate. Officially, many Negroes do not exist. Thousands do not even appear on the national census.

It has been argued that many Americans have completely

* "The Negro Family: the Case for Action" by Daniel P. Moynihan, published by the US Department of Labour.

failed to understand the nature of the problems of the cities: that they assume that race is at the root of the ghetto situation, while, in fact, economics alone account for a great deal. The Negro in the Northern city is only the last in a long series of generations of under-privileged immigrants who have been coming to America since the nineteenth century, and who have progressively moved on to better things, leaving their wretched houses for their successors. Thus it is argued that but for the great Negro migrations from the South in two World Wars, the city slums would still be causing overwhelming problems, merely that their occupants would be of white Middle-European stock instead of black. This argument can be reinforced by pointing to past great riots and turmoil in American cities—particularly those involving the Irish in the early years of this century.

But it is difficult to say just how far all this is relevant. There is overwhelming evidence to indicate the part racial discrimination has played in preventing the city Negro from finding a self-respecting job, or even one that enables him to live above the national poverty level of 3,000 dollars a year. The Vietnam war has emphasised one aspect of employment desperation, with Negroes re-enlisting in the army at the end of their term of duty at a far higher rate than whites: fighting the war with the army can offer them more than fighting their own war within their own country. It is extraordinarily difficult for a Negro to get a bank loan to start his own business; since the riots it is hard even to get insurance for property in ghetto areas. De facto school segregation makes a reasonable education a luxury, and another factor which makes the army so attractive to ambitious Negroes is that for many, the GI education bill provides their only chance to get a college education, which is available almost free once they have completed their service.

And yet one is still only scratching the surface of the problems within the ghettoes. Their ever-increasing complexity makes every measure designed to solve them almost obsolete by the time it is devised.

The greatest social development in America since the war has been the vast migration of the middle-class whites out of the city centres into the suburbs, indeed this process began very many years ago. Because of the nation's fiscal system, this has meant that hundreds of thousands of those whose taxes should be working to improve conditions in the cities now live outside the tax boundaries, and only come into the city during the day to work—contributing nothing. Those left, so many of them in the ghettoes, are barely within taxable limits. The result has been quite simple : most of America's cities are in desperate financial straits at a time when more money is needed more badly than ever before. It is a crisis that is as yet unresolved. Among the obvious approaches, financial aid on a massive scale from the Federal government (if Congress will vote the money) seems the only answer in the short term, although some mayors, like John Lindsay in New York, have been considering measures like a tax on commuters who work in their cities by day. In the longer term, the more serious question must be answered : should the cities and states have a far greater degree of fiscal independence, enabling them to deal with problems at a local level, instead of via far-away Washington? But that is an issue stretching over decades, not just years.

So many of the attempts that have been made to cope with the cities have been either unnoticed failures or very obvious disasters. Urban renewal, the plan for renovating the slums, which has been operating in various forms since the war, became known in the ghettoes as "Negro removal". Grants for slum clearance and rebuilding would be issued, the old houses would be demolished and new ones built—and then offered for lease at vastly higher rents, far beyond the reach of the site's original occupants. Even in Washington, it became known as "Southern comfort" for the unscrupulousness with which Southern city authorities exploited its original purposes.

The worst failures and abuses of urban renewal have now been curbed, and the scheme, together with various low interest mortgage plans and loans administered by the Housing and Urban Development Department in Washington, has made some impression. But talking to house owners, local authorities and journalists in the ghettoes, it is impossible to avoid the feeling that all this is still a mere drop in the ocean when considering the scale of the problems involved. Americans fight very shy indeed of anything that smacks so much of the welfare state as government-owned housing.

In the last five years, numerous Poverty Programmes and Food Stamp programmes have sprung up from the Administration's Great Society bills. But so many of these seem to have gone the way of all hastily devised, vaguely executed schemes :

the Poverty Programme is the laughing stock of both Black and White America.

The Office of Economic Opportunity originally sought 3.4 billion dollars from the Budget Bureau for the War on Poverty in 1967. In the event, the President asked Congress for only 1.75 billion dollars, knowing that he was unlikely to get any more, and Congress actually appropriated 1.61 billion dollars. Funding the programme in 1968 has further escalated the Administration's steadily more progressive difficulties in persuading Congress to vote realistic amounts.

The War on Poverty officially began in 1964, and it has since mushroomed out into such programmes as the vocational training plan (806 million dollars granted for 1964–68), the Job Corps organisation offering education, counselling and work experience to the unemployed between the ages of 16–21 (195 million dollars spent in 1967), and the Head Start scheme for young children of under-privileged families. The last seems to date to have been far the most successful. It is aimed at taking the children of poor families at the pre-kindergarten stage and giving them the educational, medical and cultural background to be able to compete on something more like equal terms with more fortunate pupils when they start school. Under public health legislation, neighbourhood health centres have been established in some city areas lacking proper facilities. By gradual expansion of the 1935 Social Security Act, the number of those in the country entitled to public welfare has been expanded enormously, until at the end of 1967, 4.2 billion dollars were being spent on the eight million people on the welfare rolls.

Programmes like VISTA send young Americans to under-privileged areas to do social work as a kind of domestic Peace Corps. And the Food Stamp programme enables the poor to buy stamps at a low price which when presented in the shops can purchase a much higher value in food (this is partly intended to prevent money being spent on non-essentials as might be the case if hard cash was handed out). Other programmes distribute basic food necessities in poverty-stricken areas— although many county authorities around the country have had to be pressured very hard indeed to agree to distribute the parcels, this notably in the South.

Set out in the above manner, however, the Administration's

Great Society programmes sound far-reaching, imaginative, and generous. But the gulf between the theory and the execution since 1964 has proved a very painful one. More than that, a parsimonious Congress has consistently reduced the appropriations the Administration has requested for its plans, until many of them reach only a fraction of the people they must in order to succeed. In 1966, the Census Bureau computed that forty-one per cent of all non-whites were living below the official poverty level, as against twelve per cent of all whites. The poverty programmes would need a dozen times their present funds to make a real impact on these figures.

Nevertheless, so much of the money that has been granted has disappeared in ill-conceived short-term plans, or worse, lost for lack of any plan at all, that many observers see distinct ceilings on the practical possibilities of what could be achieved even if endless money was available.

The economist Walter Heller claims that even if the Vietnam war, with its 30 billion or so dollars a year drain on the economy, ended tomorrow, it would be impossible in practical terms to channel more than a very limited proportion of this into the war on poverty. And those optimists who see an end of the war as hailing the start of vastly greater expenditure on domestic problems ignore the Congress : that body, which was so stubbornly resistant to a ten per cent income tax surcharge, is merely likely to regard an end of the war as a chance to give middle-class America its third colour TV sets.

In almost every American city, one can find dozens of odd organisations working in various ways on ghetto and racial problems, sometimes financed by foundations like Ford or Rockefeller, sometimes with local money, sometimes a Federal grant. There are some extremely able, not to say deeply committed minds working with many of these groups. Some of the ideas with which they are experimenting seem far-sighted. But the degree of fragmentation, lack of co-ordination, and often just plain irrelevance makes it all seem to add up once again to too little too late. At an organisation like Jobs Now in Chicago, financed by a Federal grant, groups of young Negroes are being taught some skills, given lectures on subjects like family budgeting, personal appearance, behaviour at job interviews, and are then assisted to find jobs. But the truculence and indifference of many of their students ensures that only a small percentage of those taking part will even bother to complete the course properly A report on progress issued in the autumn of 1967 showed that of 1,218 who enrolled for the programme, 308 are now employed. This in itself is no mean achievement, considering the temperament and case history of many of those the organisation takes on. But to leave the Jobs Now office and take a walk through the city's South Side is only to find a feeling of hopelessness: Chicago needs an organisation like Jobs Now —but a hundred times the size and scope to make any real impact on conditions which lead to misery and violence.

In Chicago alone, a 1966 study by the Association of Commerce and Industry showed that the median family income in the city's ten most impoverished areas was 4,810 dollars a year as against an average of 8,100 dollars a year for the city as a whole, and 9,400 for the metropolitan area. Between 1960 and 1966, average family purchasing power in these ghetto areas increased only five per cent as against sixteen per cent for the metropolitan area as a whole. Twenty-seven per cent of all persons in the ten chosen neighbourhoods were on public assistance, compared with the seven per cent average for the city. And six of the ten poverty areas had 30,000 inhabitants per square mile compared with the city's average density of 15,000.

If this is the stage on which the drama of the American cities' crisis is being played, it is no more encouraging to look at the situation of the actors. The only difference between old and young is that as always, the old are more willing, despite the misery of the status quo, to accept it. For the young Negro in the ghetto, the outlook is very different. He can look at his family, probably composed of at least four or five brothers and sisters, and see a father who if he is still at home at all, has long ago abandoned the struggle to carve out a higher place in a hostile society. His own hero may be Stokeley Carmichael or Rap Brown, the latter with his famous wolfish remark: "Violence is as American as apple pie!" He probably belongs to a street gang, and may well walk armed. There is a good chance he has been in trouble with the police, even if he does not actually have a record of convictions. His family certainly has a television set on which every night he can watch the glossy soap operas of America presented with its Hollywood sets. And they may well have a car (one feature of American society's status-seeking which the Negro has discovered and seized on is the importance of possesion of a large car and a television set, even if the family are sleeping four to a room). Since he has probably dropped out of school and, if he has a job at all, it is very unlikely to be a skilled one, he has plenty of free time, and on summer evenings when the heat is unbearable, in a crowded house without air-conditioning or reasonable ventilation, there is little else to do but walk the streets—or just sit on the fire escape waiting for something to happen. These past two summers, there has not been long to wait.

In a famous remark which rapidly travelled across America, because it said what much of America wanted to believe, Whitney Young of the Urban League organisation said: "Stokeley Carmichael has a following of 50 Negroes and 500 white reporters." Carmichael's violent pronouncements receive so much publicity, his movements such endless scrutiny, that it is unquestionable that the American press have done much to make him the national figure he is. It is also undoubtedly true that the majority of American Negroes want nothing to do with Carmichael or his ideas—such of them as, at heart, he believes in himself. But Whitney Young was wrong because Carmichael —"Stokeley baby!" as he is known in the ghettoes—is the classic case of a figure who if he did not exist, would have to have been created.

He advocates violence—or more precisely, armed revolt—as the means of achieving Negro freedom. He believes not in an integrated society of black and white, but in a totally separate Negro existence. He does not bother with practicalities, but he has discovered that Whitey is in the mood to be impressed when he urges the "soul brothers" to get themselves guns and break out once and for all. With a thinly-veiled note of anti-semitism in his preaching (as among many Black Power leaders, playing on ghetto belief that they are being exploited by white Jewish shopkeepers), and his lack of concern for reason, he seems basically more of an anarchist than anything else.

But what is more important, he is also the very articulate spokesman for hundreds of thousands of young Negroes all over America, and for a cause they believe in implicitly. It is irrelevant whether his views are irresponsible, illogical, impossible. What matters is that there are significant numbers of Negroes who agree with them. It seems pointless to waste much time on Stokeley Carmichael, the man, because his interest and importance stems from the view he represents, not because he himself has anything remarkable to offer.

Carmichael is harmless—contrary to the belief of most white Americans—simply because he moves constantly in the spot-light. It is what is going on behind Carmichael, among figures in the ghetto of whom no one but a handful of journalists and social workers have ever heard, that is far more significant. It concerns the whole issue of the American Negro's search for an identity, perhaps the most vital aspect of the racial situation in 1968.

At the United Church of Christ in Detroit, a few blocks from 12th Street, centre of the 1967 riots, the Rev. Albert Cleage preaches every Sunday to a packed congregation of very well-dressed looking Negroes. Cleage himself is a Negro, although he could easily be mistaken for a white. He is an extremely amusing man who, like so many Black Nationalists, has a casually wolfish sense of humour which is charming because his manner belies the completely ruthless substance of what he is saying. He con-ducts his services along undeviatingly Christian lines, in a church where the only initially startling feature is the huge figure of the Messiah painted above the altar behind him—it is black. One is charmed by the tiny child soloist who sings a spiritual between prayers, by the friendliness of the middle-aged women who act as his ushers, by the enthusiasm of the congregation's hymn singing. But then hear Cleage preach a sermon: watch him stand in his pulpit for an hour or more advocating armed conflict and violence as the only means of achieving racial equality. His audience are completely gripped: "Preach it, baby!" "Tell it to 'em as it is!" "Yeaah, brother!" Cleage is a brilliant demagogue, very obviously a highly intelli-gent man, and most of all, three-quarters of what he says is completely true.

"You know what the difference is between the situation now and the situation two years ago? Well, two years ago we were frightened. And now we ain't frightened any more. It ain't us that's scared now—it's Whitey! They talk to us about riots; have they forgotten that they had their revolution too? Don't they spend all their time talking about that time they threw all the tea in Boston Harbour? In Detroit every constitutional right has been denied to black citizens! All the power of the Constitution has been thrown into protecting *white* power and *white* supremacy! Just as they talked about protecting law and order, they themselves were destroying that same law and order! If you are black and you think your concern is with law and order, you are either craven selfish or insane!"

After the service, meet some of "the Reverend's" friends in the hall below the church: two brothers, lawyers, who are running a movement dedicated to the creation of a separate Negro state in Louisiana, Georgia, Alabama, "and we're prepared to negotiate about Florida . . ." There are representatives from the Los Angeles US movement, there is a mixture of large anonymous figures hanging around in the background who say little but look much. Cleage himself, charming as ever, says that even if he is stockpiling arms under the altar, he'd hardly be likely to say so, would he?

Half a continent away, in Los Angeles, Maulana Ron Karenga is the founder and leader of the US movement, who with their shorn heads, grey smocks, effigies around the neck and sun-glasses on the eyes, look very dangerous indeed.

"Power is not granted. It is taken," says Karenga. "Don't please talk about 'the situation in your country'. This is not my country. What do we seek? Self-determination, self-defence and self-respect."

The US movement is probably the most articulate of all those around the United States which, in a search for "our own sociology, mythology, economic structure and culture", has turned back to look to Africa. They hold study seminars on African culture. They talk of civil disorders not as "riots", but as "the revolt". Karenga's idol was Malcolm X, the Black Muslim leader who was murdered in 1965. He describes Malcolm as "the perfect man". Again like so many Black Nationalist movements, US has an air of religious mystique about it, although Karenga says: "It is up to us to solve our problems. Prayer solves nothing." His followers learn to speak Swahili, call Africans "soul brother", but say they are better off than the African in having no tribe, and hence being more flexible.

And once again, the dry humour: "Do we get any money from whites? Who cares, man? It's all green when it comes . . ."

Cleage and Ron Karenga and a hundred or more others like them all over America, are the spearhead of a new kind of segregation movement: towards black segregation. In despair, in impotence, they have rejected the idea of integration into white society as undesirable, because, perhaps, at the bottom of very proud spirits, they do not see themselves achieving it. They have turned instead to a search for pride within themselves and within their race—"black is beautiful!" has become one of the soul cries of the ghetto. They rejoice in having made Whitey fear them, because if you cannot find respect, fear is the next best thing. And yet, when the chips are down, although they would never admit it, perhaps not even to themselves—they will not lead the armed revolt seeking triumph through violence. After Martin Luther King was assassinated Ron Karenga toured the Watts district of Los Angeles urging the young, in their vicious anger, to "keep your cool, baby!" Like so much in the ghettoes in 1968, even an admonition has an exclamation mark on the end.

Men like Karenga and Cleage are too intelligent to think that a serious revolt in the cities could ever work. Many people are already very frightened lest some riot break out in which attacks were made on a white area: in that event, considering the terrifyingly hysterical temperament in many white city suburbs, where every house has a gun, something approaching a massacre could occur. Not of the whites either. But fortunately, for such an attack to take place, a complete break with the present pattern of ghetto riots would be required, and there seems nothing to suggest that this will take place.

What Karenga and Cleage and the others are doing is something which in the long run, may be of inestimable value to America: they are teaching young Negroes to "walk tall". Perhaps one cannot fully understand what this means unless one has never been able to do it.

The tragedy of the more violent aspects of the Nationalist creed is that the disciples believe more implicitly than the teachers. Here, now and today, the symptoms and the results of this transition are causing acute problems. Most white Americans have only just adjusted to the idea that integration is a cause not only worth fighting towards, but a national necessity. Now, like a slap in the face, they have been told that many Negroes are not interested in integration any more. Blacks demand that in Negro schools, only Negroes teach, cook, clean —even service the heating plant. At universities, Negroes do not want to hear about John Paul Jones, they want courses in

Negro history, African culture. Many have adopted the smocks or shaven heads of the Black Muslims, disdaining collar, tie and business suit. Greet a friend in the street, clench your fist and say: "Black Power, baby!" This to many white Americans is a cause of not only bewilderment but anger. "Where have we gone wrong? What can we do?" So many times that question has been asked in 1968.

In the last resort, it is clear that even if created at the behest of the Negro American himself (and one reiterates again that many more Negroes attend meetings of the moderate civil rights National Association for the Advancement of Coloured People than of US or similar movements) a separate black society cannot work. But despite all the short and even medium term problems it has created, Black Nationalism may accomplish an enormous amount in dragging the Negro from the despair, the apathy, the negativism into which generations of hopeless humiliation had cast him.

One of the most fascinating stories of Black America in 1968 was that of Alex Haley, a Negro journalist who helped to write *The Autobiography of Malcolm X* and is, improbably, chief interviewer for *Playboy* magazine. In five years of research, Haley, by a mixture of fantastic luck and inspired hard work, managed to trace his family history not only back to slave days, but back to Africa as well. He traced white ancestors in Ireland to the plantation in the South where their casual use of the Negro women bred white blood into almost every Negro in America. He followed an old family story to the West Coast of Africa. He searched the records of slave ships in Lloyd's Register. At the end of it all, Alex Haley has achieved what every Negro in America is searching to do: he has found a past. Symbolically, his contribution to the race's culture may prove of deep significance to Black America today. But this is the positive aspect of Nationalism. There is another, more sensitive, more difficult side.

Roy Wilkins, director of the long-established NAACP* is an Uncle Tom. Whitney Young is an Uncle Tom. Ralph Bunche, Deputy Secretary-General of the United Nations, is an Uncle Tom. Thurogood Marshall of the Supreme Court is the biggest Uncle Tom of all. . . . This is the other side of the battle for

* National Association for the Advancement of Coloured People.

identification—the total rejection of the Negro who "makes it" within the white power structure.

As in their very different ways, Cleage, Karenga and Alex Haley make their contributions to pride in blackness for its own sake, no one is more vilified by the young ghetto Negro than a man like Senator Edward Brooke of Massachusetts. Brooke was a young Negro lawyer of middle-class origins who became one of the most successful state Attorney-Generals in Massachusetts history. From there, he went on to the Senate, where he is a highly intelligent, moderate liberal Republican, with a special interest in foreign affairs. Brooke knows as well as any man that nearly half the city Negroes in America currently derive most of their income from one or another form of welfare benefits. He is personally acquainted with most civil rights leaders. But although he was a member of the Riot Commission last year, he has refused to become deeply involved in Negro affairs. His argument is that he was elected to represent the State of Massachusetts. He was not, he says, elected by them for the purpose of leading civil rights demonstrations (the value of which he is doubtful about anyway), or to champion the cause of his race. Brooke thus becomes, to the young Negro on the streets of Detroit, a traitor to his race. Who can decide what the obligations of identification are to be?

Communication, education, identification . . . the three keys to unlocking the crisis in the ghettoes. One of the tragedies of 1968 was the story of the Report of the President's Commission on Civil Disorders, established by President Johnson in the late summer of 1967 to consider the riots in the cities. The Report was published in March, 1968, and was considered by almost everyone in any way involved with the crisis of the cities to be the most comprehensive, far-reaching, reasonable document on the situation ever produced. It is pointless to dwell at length on the Report's post-publication history : sufficient to say that its recommendations called for action on a gigantic scale to deal with slums, find jobs and alter the character of the nation's cities. Congress considered what it would cost, laughed and turned to other matters. The President, a politician, considered whether it was practicable, decided apparently that it was not, and made no comment of any serious nature on the Report. The nation, much of whom, according to the polls, already consider that the Negro is being given too much too fast, saw visions of some vast hand-out scheme on an unprecedented scale which would raise taxes considerably. The nation shrugged its shoulders and forgot the report.

Among the Report's main conclusions : many of those killed in the 1967 riots, died because of indiscriminate and irresponsible action by troops and police. Much of the "sniping" alleged to have taken place appeared to be the result of troops mistaking each other's fire for that of the enemy. The authorities in almost every city displayed a remarkable talent for doing the worst possible thing at the worst possible time. Fear is the key, and fear drove many people to many things. It is perhaps worth adding that after the riots of April, 1968, the American press praised the authorities concerned for acting with restraint and discretion. And yet to any eyewitness, it still seems incredible that the National Guard are being unleashed, heavily armed, very frightened and with less proper training and leadership than the average Boy Scout, to handle a situation in which so many scars must remain long after the shooting has stopped.

The Report also emphasised the total feeling of alienation in the ghetto which has led to disbelief in almost everything Whitey says. Word of mouth is the only respected means of communication with the ghetto, with the result that dangerous incidents are constantly provoked by the hive of rumour that exists. The report quoted one interviewer who said :

"The average black person couldn't give less of a damn about what the media say. The intelligent black person is resentful at what he considers to be a totally false portrayal of what goes on in the ghetto. Most black people see the newspapers as mouthpieces of the 'power structure'."

Thus, yet another hazard further confuses a tangled web : the loss of faith in what is said by any but your own kind. And of your own kind, who is there to listen to? One of the most pathetic little corners of American society is that created by successful Negroes; those few who have made it, in business or professionally, are so terrified of losing what they have gained that they establish their own pattern of life, modelled on, but separate from, their white equals. Worst of all, completely separate from that of their black former social equals. They have their houses and their pets, their tea parties and their dinner parties—even in some cities their own debutante season. The latter phenomenon is obviously restricted to the very rarified group who have made a very great deal of money indeed : but between these and the ghettoes is a much larger structure of small businessmen, barbers and shopkeepers who make, perhaps, 15,000 dollars a year, own a small reasonably modern house in their own little corner of the suburbs, and at all costs avoid entangling themselves with those whom they fear might drag them back to the wretchedness from which they have escaped. To whom, therefore, does this leave the leadership in the ghettoes? To the gang leaders, some priests, a few white social workers and men like Cleage and Ron Karenga.

It is in this context that one can become in some ways more surprised that the Riot Report concluded that there was no evidence of the riots having been deliberately organised. There is something to suggest that some individuals and groups exploited riot situations once started, but most riots have begun because of some relatively commonplace incident which occurred at a time when numbers of hot, aggressive, frustrated young people were in a mood to tear the hell out of something.

Is it really so remarkable that the rioters burn their own areas? They burn shops which in many cases have been openly exploiting them. They burn homes which they not only do not love, but which they dream of escaping from. And most of all, they literally seize with both hands the opportunity to take what they cannot have any other way : colour television sets, clothes, washing machines, furniture . . . America is the land of the hard sell. The residents of the ghetto who watch television hour after hour, every day, are bombarded, battered, goaded, tempted, with images of objects which they are told are highly desirable, but which they cannot have. Such possessions as they do have are probably bought on hire purchase, and the head of the family's income is almost certainly shattered by the weight of credit debts. This, they are told from the first hour of life in which they can hear, is "The Great Society". It is a society with so much surplus production that it has invented an electric pencil sharpener, electric letter opener, electric carving knife. This is the most fantastic carrot ever dangled before the most angry and bewildered donkey in human history. On April 6th, 1968, I saw the donkey kicking.

In order to consider first the racial crisis in the Northern cities, I have rather upset the chronology of the event of the first week in April. The riots in Chicago, Washington and elsewhere reflected Negro fury arising from the tragedy that took place on the evening of Thursday, April 4th. I was in Washington, watching television, when the first bulletin flashed over the air announcing that Martin Luther King had been shot in Memphis, Tennessee. Not many minutes later came confirmation that he was dead. Memphis is only a short flight from the nation's capital, but it takes one into another world: the world supposedly of Gone With The Wind *and Scarlett O'Hara, and more recently of a hatred and injustice that the work of men like King was thought to have done much to alleviate. King was a man out of the South, who had achieved his national prominence for his efforts in the South. On April 4th, he died in the South, and in the first breath of contact with Memphis it quickly became clear just how much he left that still desperately needs to be changed.*

CHAPTER 3

ANOTHER LOST GENERATION

"What the hell have them damn nigras got to complain about, anyways?"
A white man in Memphis, April 5th, 1968

Funny thing about Memphis, nobody really thought it was much of a town until April 4th, 1968. Now, if it had been Jackson, Mississippi, for instance, or Montgomery, Alabama . . . Then everybody could have nodded wisely and said: "It had to happen here". But Memphis was just a decaying, second-rate road junction at the top of the Mississippi Delta which nobody gave a damn about. Its main daily paper, the *Commercial Appeal,* had been trying a little liberalism in the spirit of an English tourist abroad experimenting with goat's eyes on toast. The majority of its white population appeared to be passively rather than actively segregationist. The mayor, Henry Loeb, seemed to regard stubbornness as a virtue second only to plain rudeness.

It is highly questionable whether Martin Luther King was right to be in Memphis in the first place. His advent was originally prompted by a strike of the city garbage collectors for recognition as a union and higher pay. A complex of side-issues became woven into the situation, including the question of whether public employees had a right to strike (vide the New York garbage strike a few weeks earlier), and most significant of all, race. Ninety-eight per cent of the strikers were Negroes. It was inevitable that their dispute should become a racial row.

But given conditions in Memphis and given the reputation of Dr. King, it seems at least possible that the strike might have been more easily settled by leverage from behind the scenes than by a protest march which, even had it not ended in disorder, was certain to have brought out the worst in the white authorities. Sure enough, when Dr. King, on his departure from the city after the march and subsequent trouble, was abused by Mayor Loeb with stupid and taunting words, the garbage strike had escalated to a point where neither side was likely to back down. King returned to the fray, taking up residence in the Lorraine Motel—a building somewhat representative of the city in sleaziness and appearance. During King's previous visit, a reporter had remarked needlingly on the expense of the hotel in which he was staying, so this time he settled for humbler quarters.

Despite all that was said in the horrified days following April 4th, Martin Luther King was probably achieving less at the time he went to Memphis than in any previous phase of his life. That is not to say that he had lost popularity with the vast mass of American Negroes. The splinter movements of militants only account for a small fraction of the total black population, and King that April was, for almost all his people, still the natural leader. On the wall of a Negro home in the ghettoes of Detroit or Chicago, one would probably find three pictures: of Jesus Christ, John F. Kennedy and Martin Luther King.

But even King could not escape the fact that it is very much easier to change what is written than to change what is only sensed. In the South, his long succession of marches and protests, sit-downs and meetings in the late '50s and early '60s achieved an enormous amount in breaking down the legal trappings of segregation, which the determination of white Southerners and the apathy of Washington had maintained for so long. But this done, what can a stroke of the pen do to make a Jackson Negro able to afford the money to eat in the restaurants where he is now legally acceptable? What can a Government in Washington do to prevent the voters of Georgia from properly electing a governor, even though he is an open champion of segregation, and rather delicately poised between reason and mental unbalance?

Martin Luther King had, when he went to Memphis, almost completely torn down the stone walls in the South. He was being faced instead with battles against a kind of gas cloud: you can smell it, you can feel it polluting the air. But how do you blow it away? In the early evening of April 4th, as he stood on the balcony of the Lorraine Motel talking to his aides about plans for his next march, it was a problem he had not satisfactorily resolved. He was only 204 feet from the smallest window of a dirty tenement building across the street.

* * *

Memphis, Tennessee, ten hours later, was a city frightened and silent, ashamed but vile-mouthed. Seeing a major city in a civilised country under curfew for the first time is a chilling experience. America is close enough to home to make one imagine say, Birmingham or Manchester with deserted streets and armoured personnel carriers roaring past the shops. It is even more depressing to find the men who supposedly control the situation nervous and jumpy: a police patrolman who stopped our taxi on the way in from the airport to ask our business was jittery enough to make the driver remark: "He's too scared to be carrying a gun on the downtown detail today."

Sporadic violence had flickered throughout the night: looting of liquor stores (always a prime target in any major city disorder), one or two incidents of sniping, some rock-throwing and casual destruction. But the National Guard had been summoned early, the police were out in force and control had been restored without great difficulty. Not that the Negroes of Memphis seemed especially roused for a riot: come the dawn, and the black faces on the streets looked much more stunned than vengeful. Ironically, and yet inevitably, it was the whites who were contributing the hate. A waitress in the coffee house where I had breakfast was furious that the nation was lowering its flags to half mast to honour King: "He weren't no President or nuthin'!" A taxi driver who took me to the shabby funeral parlour, where in macabre but customary style, King's body was being patched up for its public lying-in-state, remarked bitterly: "The city fathers tell us there's only thirty-eight per cent nigras in this city, but it looks to me more like there was about sixty. Just what the hell have them damn nigras got to complain about, anyways? They've appointed a nigra judge and the nigra children got better schools than our kids—they ain't got one damn thing to moan about. And just how the hell did they let a goddam garbage strike develop into something like this?"

Few people, white or black, ventured on to the streets until late into the day. Small groups of police were scattered at intervals on the corners and at intervals the quiet was shattered by two or more patrol cars screaming on their way to some violent errand. Already, the questions were being asked as to how an assassin who had fired on King from such close range could have escaped when there were so many police in the vicinity. The answer was simple : in unprofessional, very human style, they had run not to the source of the shot, but towards the bleeding victim, when they saw King fall. A trail of conflicting and confusing evidence marked the assumed escape route of the killer, who had made his break in the confusion. When the Attorney-General, Ramsay Clark, flew into the city from Washington later in the day promising an "early arrest", his optimism already seemed distinctly premature.*

At the Lorraine Motel, below the balcony on which King had been shot, the Reverend Ralph Abernathy, the man he had appointed to succeed him before his death, held a press conference that morning. Abernathy looked subdued and unhappy. It was King's other aides, Jesse Jackson, Andrew Young, Hosea Williams and the others, who were doing what talking was possible that day. There was Mrs. Coretta King, flying from her home in Atlanta to collect her dead husband's body in a plane provided by Bobby Kennedy, immediately provoking suggestions that he was trying to exploit tragedy for his own political ends. And as always that week, there was television. How many times in 1968 did television hold one mesmerised for days on end, unwilling to hear or see more, but frightened to switch off for fear of missing something? If those of us in Memphis were watching television, with its tributes and its reflections, and its haunting news-clippings of King in his life, how much more so were millions of other Americans all over the country. It is strange that a medium which America has successfully reduced to the lowest common denominator should still have the power to evoke so much emotion. And never so irrelevant in its commercialism as that week, with an advertisement for sexier toothpaste or more powerful deodorant seeming to punctuate every bulletin of tragedy and history. To watch television in America at moments great or small, is to believe that this is a country obsessed only with indigestion and BO.

The coming of evening, after a sickening day in which the

* James Ray, or Galt, or Sneyd, was arrested in London on June 8th, 1968, on suspicion of involvement in the assassination of King.

anger of almost every white in Memphis seemed to stem solely from a feeling that their city's "good name" had been sullied—somehow by the behaviour of "the nigras"—brought only a new fear. How easy it is for a few angry men of any colour to frighten a whole city! There was no riot that night, just a rattle of gunfire every now and again, which blazed up and died away in a few seconds. A lone sniper would fire a few rounds at something or perhaps at nothing at all, and then melt away into the darkness before the flashing lights of the patrol cars were even in sight. There can only have been a handful of guerillas on the streets of Memphis that night and their activities were only spasmodic all weekend. But if such a handful so wished, they could keep a city on its nerve-ends almost indefinitely. I couldn't help wondering when someone would decide to try it.

Back at the hotel, once more in front of the television, once more hearing the reports of violence and fury that sent American housewives to learn how to shoot a pistol and policemen to city halls demanding armoured cars and machine guns to maintain law and order; someone was remarking: "Funny that this should all have started in the South; I mean, the South has been so quiet this last year or two . . ."

*   *   *

From soon after the Second World War until the early 1960s, the Negro struggle to achieve an integrated society in America's South received wider publicity around the world than almost any other aspect of the nation's domestic affairs. Perhaps seldom in recent history has there been a battle fought in which the moral issues seemed so clear cut: in the midst of the richest country on earth, one sector of the population was fighting viciously to deny the other basic human rights. The fact that the Southern Negro has accomplished so much between 1945 and 1968 has had nothing to do with any weakening of will on the part of the segregationists. It is simply that as in the American Civil War, the South has found itself opposed by forces too strong to resist indefinitely. The segregationists, accepting tactical withdrawals where necessary, have been forced back to fight a quieter but in no way less stubborn war of guerilla actions. The Ku Klux Klan lynchings, which extended into the 1930s and '40s, have been virtually eliminated; the law allows Negroes untrammelled admittance to all public facilities and schools;

and many of the most infamous police chiefs and state governors are now mere historical curiosities.

Everyone who was old enough to read a newspaper at the time, remembers the 1954 landmark in civil rights history when the United States Supreme Court decreed that school segregation was unconstitutional and must cease. The world recalls the days when Eisenhower dispatched troops to Little Rock, Arkansas, to protect Negro students, when Martin Luther King leapt to national prominence as leader of the Negro boycott on the buses of Montgomery, Alabama, and when Robert F. Kennedy as Attorney-General battered a path for the Negro "Freedom Ride" demonstration through the South.

The laws changed . . . and the riots in the Northern cities gradually pushed the South back into its old obscurity. The headline-catching confrontations between blacks and whites take place in the North now : perhaps that is why the whites of Memphis reacted so viciously when the assassination of Martin Luther King once more directed the spotlight on old wounds, if only for as long as it takes to kill a man and bury him.

I was in Memphis for a memorial march held four days after King's assassination; from there, the drama moved to Atlanta, Georgia, for his funeral. And from Atlanta, long after America's attention had switched back to elections, riots and Vietnam, I found myself travelling across the heart of the South—from Montgomery, Alabama, to Jackson, Mississippi, from Jackson to New Orleans, Lousiana, then into Texas and up again once more to Little Rock, Arkansas.

It is one of the most depressing journeys in the world : not because the South is scenically ugly, on the contrary, it is one of the most beautiful parts of America. It is because somehow I had taken it for granted that when King died, he had died leaving the South far better off than when he and his colleagues were born into it. Those who know the South well, and have known it for many years, say that one is wrong to be too gloomy because it is incredible what has been accomplished in the past twenty years. But it is difficult to be impressed when first, one still sees all around one evidence of human misery which makes the Negro of the ghetto seem almost fortunate. And secondly and more important, when talking to the whites of the South about anything more controversial than the charms of a mint julep, it seems like listening to creatures from another planet.

If Memphis was a foretaste of the Southern White, try sampling the beliefs of Lester Maddox, the Governor of Georgia: "Martin Luther King contributed more to violence than any man in the United States". "Yes, I believe in segregation. I believe every man should have a choice as to whether he is to live in an integrated society or not" (Maddox closed down a restaurant he owned in Atlanta rather than obey the law and integrate it). "Our state has as good a reputation as any in our country." It was one of Maddox' aides who was seen to lean out of his state-house window during King's funeral and yell: "You know what they're going to do when they catch Martin Luther King's killer? Fine him fifteen dollars for shootin' coons out of season!"

A businessman in Montgomery, Alabama, spent twenty minutes trying to convince me that Martin Luther King was leading the civil rights movement in the South for personal financial gain. He went on to tell a series of ingeniously crude stories about the supposed personal life of the Reverend Ralph Abernathy, King's successor. His conversation was not untypical, his approach only slightly less subtle than that of most white Southerners I met. I am told that had I visited the South as a tourist rather than as a journalist, I might have enjoyed my stay more. But while this may be true, I can't see how it could reflect greater credit on the people.

Perhaps one small point helps to put the South in perspective: in the Riot Report of March 1968, the Commission criticised a Newark, New Jersey, policeman who flew the old Confederate flag on his car. He was considered to be gratuitously and provocatively insulting the Negro area in which he operated.

But during my own first days in the South, I saw dozens of cars wearing the Confederate emblem in place of a front number plate. I saw the State Capitol of Alabama flying the Confederate flag in place of the United States flag. I had bought a towel bearing the Confederate flag myself, but when a friend toured several Atlanta department stores the next day in search of a similar one, he was told they were no longer stocked. One shop revealed that an organisation called the Daughters of the Confederacy had put on pressure to withdraw the towels on the grounds that they dishonoured the flag. The organisation, it seemed, enjoyed sufficient popular support to be listened to. The honour of the Confederacy was saved.

Many southerners, unbelievably, still seem to see themselves as Rhett Butlers or Scarlett O'Haras, fighting some noble rear-guard action to save what has Gone with the Wind. These are not the people who tell dirty stories about Civil Rights leaders in bars. They are merely those reared in a strong tradition—not so much of retaining or being nostalgic about slavery as such, rather of honouring the ideals of chivalry and independence which they believe went hand in hand with the plantation economy of the old South. They do not hate Negroes—it is the poor whites who supply most of the hate. They merely believe that to preserve their proud society, they must keep an ordered social system : one "ordered" in that the Negro stays in his usual place. They deeply resent the Federal Government's interference in local affairs, and while they may not hold George Wallace in high personal regard, they will vote for him.

If this nostalgia sounds improbable, I should add that one of the commonest sights in the South is that of new houses going up, built rigidly on plantation mansion lines. Surrounded by their magnolias and their well-kept gardens, half a dozen of these elegantly columned homes standing side by side make a wonderful picture. It is only when one drives a mile or two down the road that the image is shattered : when one sees other southerners, very many of them living in squalid shacks that if seen in England would be the subject of a major newspaper exposé.

These are some of the sights and sounds of the South in 1968, seemingly so much quieter than those of the ghetto, so much less threatening to the white middle classes. The old Negro couple sitting in their rocking chairs on the porch just before sunset have none of the impact of the ugly street corner gang on 12th Street, Detroit. The local church meeting in memory of Martin Luther King will go unnoticed by the white community, and thus unfeared. The white civil rights worker in a small town in Mississippi no longer has to walk in fear of his life : he is only required to live in total isolation from the whites, not by law or decree, simply because he is not wanted. He is ignored.

Before considering the South economically or politically, it is important to accept that there are many problems which go deeper than racial hatred alone. The South's era of prosperity began at the end of the eighteenth century with the invention of the cotton gin, when the slave system provided massive cheap labour and English textile factories cried out for as much raw material as America could provide. But when the Confederacy's defeat in the Civil War ended slavery, so also did it destroy the economy on which the South was based. Between the 1860s and the early years of this century, the population both white and black eked a kind of living from the land. Then, with the First World War and the demand for cheap labour in the Northern factories, the first of the great Negro migrations from the South began. This movement has greatly slowed in present times, and more important, the agriculture of the South has been given a tremendous boost by the coming of mechanisation. Mechanisation has helped to make many Southern landowners richer than ever before. But it has also made redundant many of those, both white and black, whom the land hitherto sustained.

The result has been a classic circle : there is still little industry in many areas (Atlanta and a few other big cities being notable exceptions), and yet how can industry be attracted to an area where all the available labour is hopelessly unskilled? Poor non-landowning whites have, for years, managed only marginally better than some Negroes, which largely accounts for their resistance to better status for Negroes—a terror of being overtaken. Poor whites' education and training is often little greater. The only thing that many poor white and Negroes have in common in the South is that economically they are relatively worse off than twenty years ago. At least twenty years ago some jobs were available.

For the Negro, there is no incentive to migrate North since his lack of skill would tell against him even more. And the Southern Negro has a far greater affinity for his home than the Negro of the North : a Southern Negro will talk with pride of being an Alabaman, loving his state in a way that at first seems incredible to an observer who has just returned from a visit to fellow-Alabaman George Wallace. The black Southerner is sustained by a religious faith, strong family ties and a long-standing sense of community. These qualities have both unified the Civil Rights movement in the South to a much greater extent than has been possible in the North, and have helped to prevent some of the violent excesses of rioting in the face of physical hardship and poverty.

But in the South eighty per cent of the non-white population earns under 4,000 dollars a year as against sixty point two per cent of non-whites at the national average. Indeed in Mississippi, sixty-six point two per cent of the Negro population earn less than 2,000 dollars a year. Only twenty-two per cent of the whites in that state earn as little as this.*

As is so often the case when considering America's problems in 1968, one is left aghast by the size and scope of the aid that would be needed to assist both Negroes and whites to make the region really viable economically, even allowing (an optimistic premise) that there was a more equitable relationship established between highly affluent landowners and miserably poor unemployed.

Against this background of an agricultural economy facing all the inevitable problems of industrialisation, set the attitudes of white Southerners and the struggle for racial integration. It is a story remarkable more than anything for how little seems to have changed since the great civil rights struggles of the '50s, and it is a story one might take up best in Atlanta—partly because my own travels began in Atlanta, but more important because Atlanta is unique in the South. It is unique for the speed of its economic growth over the past ten years or more, it is unique in being an oasis in an otherwise featureless cultural desert. It is unique in presenting the clash between the white liberals, of whom Atlanta has a considerable number, and the old guard of segregation headed by Georgia's State Governor, Lester Maddox.

Mayor Ivan Allen, who not only runs the city but is the effective leader of the progressive elements, makes no attempt to disguise his contempt for Lester Maddox. He is proud of his city's economic expansion and, even if one takes his social opinions at their most cynical value, he has a vested interest in keeping Atlanta peaceful and looking good to outside interests with thoughts of bringing in investment.

"The whites in this country," he says, "are responsible for the city ghettos and have got to do something about them, if only because we've been running the country all this time and we've allowed ghettoes to be created.

"Down here, we're making progress with education, getting more Negroes into colleges, building better schools: but the

* "The Economic Status of Negroes in the Nation and the South" by Vivian Henderson, published by the Southern Regional Council.

trouble is that so many of them go into government jobs at a national level once they're well educated. We want them owning more businesses, newspapers, radio and TV stations, so they'll have roots here.

"In the future, there has got to be greater Federal influence and Federal money in our city centres. For the moment, we're trying to achieve a compromise between maintaining law and order and preventing a blood bath. That's the problem once a riot starts—stopping it with minimum violence. But I think that if Negroes here were ripe for revolt, they'd have done so after Martin Luther King's assassination. The fact that they didn't puts us over the apex. The young are pretty restless, but if we can keep gaining time, we're making progress with houses, jobs, schools, everything. . . ."

Allen talks at a material level because he is a practical man. He knows how much is bound up with the problems of economics, housing and incomes. In 1960 there were thirty-nine per cent Negroes in Atlanta, now there are forty-four per cent. But in the last decade, Atlanta has also had the highest per cent increase in available jobs of any city in the country. The influx of big business from the North has also meant the coming of new whites—executives and managers. These people may not be desperately committed to assisting the Negro, but they lack the obduracy of the traditional white Southerner and, like Mayor Allen, they are anxious to create conditions in the city favourable for further growth. They will not sacrifice the city's interest to a particularly wretched brand of diehard politics.

The city police chief, Herbert Jenkins, plays the same tune. Fourteen per cent of his force is Negro, not an especially high percentage but getting higher. Jenkins was a member of the President's Commission which produced the Riot Report, and talking about methods of dealing with urban disorder—despite his Southern accent and old-fashioned local upbringing—he sounds a great deal more reasonable than many Washington politicians. One of the reasons he fears a riot in Atlanta is that it would almost inevitably mean summoning the National Guard to aid his men—and it would be under the control of Lester Maddox.

"Remember that Maddox is entitled to ask for help from the National Guard of a neighbouring state if he says he needs it," he added grimly. "Alabama is our neighbour. Can you imagine it? The National Guardsmen of Georgia and Alabama let loose with rifles in the Negro areas of Atlanta? It's my nightmare."

The night Martin Luther King was assassinated, Mayor Allen and Jenkins walked the streets of the Negro areas together, doing their best to see that tempers were kept under control. In 1967 while crime across the nation increased seventeen per cent, in Atlanta it increased only four per cent.

I spent a week in Atlanta, and whatever the contrary influence of Maddox and his many supporters, not to mention those in rural Georgia outside Atlanta, it seems an outstanding example of a city where economics are dictating a change in attitudes, much for the better.

There are those social commentators who know Atlanta well who laugh when the city's liberalism is cited. They claim that Atlanta has merely discovered a formula for paying devoted lip-service to liberalism while pursuing traditional policies beneath the surface. I think that Allen, Jenkins and the others, for whatever motives, are doing more than that.

It is when you take the walk to Lester Maddox' State Capitol that it becomes acutely clear how far the rural South must go before shaking off its mantle of hatred and bigotry. Maddox became Governor after a disputed election, but since his views on the racial issue seemed to differ little from those of his opponent, it is questionable whether the voters of Georgia were doing more than splitting hairs between one racist and another. He is a small, balding middle-aged figure whose past career has included picketing the White House alone as a protest against compulsory integration, and the aforementioned restaurant-owning which made him a sizeable fortune before he closed down.

"Everyone talks about what needs to be done in the United States," he says. "They ignore the accomplishments of our country. The news media spend all their time writing about beatniks, hippies and hoodlums. Our national government seems to be becoming more and more a refuge for hippies and Communists."

He is a petulant little man with a penchant for strange public remarks which have led even some of his supporters to question his mental health. The *Atlanta Constitution*, a paper nationally known for its liberal stance, often almost alone in the South, has flayed Maddox at every opportunity. But he remains Governor. He wants schools to be returned to local control to prevent their further desegregation. He wants less Federal intervention in every direction. He wants a national government which will take a nice, tough line with the Communists. It would be quite impossible to take him seriously if he was a private individual. But he is not—he is the Governor of Georgia. Is he fighting a rearguard action? Perhaps. But it is one which makes many Atlantans far prouder of their Confederate past than their developing present.

When Martin Luther King's funeral took place in the city five days after his assassination, Maddox shut himself and his wife in his state house with a hundred and sixty state troopers. And while the city authorities won their battle not to have National Guardsmen on duty in the city centre that day, they were kept on stand-by close to hand. There were many whites in Atlanta who anticipated that with so many thousands of Negro mourners gathered together, violent trouble was inescapable. It was a tribute both to the city and to the Negro community who had lost so much that the occasion passed off in complete dignity. For Atlanta, as Mayor Allen remarked, the apex seems to have been passed. Knowing the city heightens all the more the feeling of desolation as one leaves it—moving westward.

Just before I left, an American Civil Liberties Union lawyer remarked bitterly: "Maddox, sitting locked up with his troops on funeral day, was the only honest white man in the south. It's what they'd all have done if they could." In neighbouring Alabama, they don't need to. Whether the death of Governor Lurleen Wallace, resulting in George Wallace's loss of any official stranglehold on the state, will make any difference to his effective powers, it is too early to tell. But there is no doubt about the ease with which Alabamans are maintaining the segregated status quo without actually having to break any laws to do it.

At a Palm Sunday service in Montgomery, the state's capital, in memory of Martin Luther King, there were perhaps a hundred whites to six thousand Negroes. The integration of the school system, as in so many other parts of the South, has been on a strictly token basis. The choices offered in the state elections are such that the Negro community were advised by civil rights workers and their own leaders to vote a straight Democratic ticket—which included voting for Lurleen Wallace—simply because the alternative candidates were even worse. There is still almost total church segregation : indeed, one of the most fascinating aspects of segregation is the manner in which many white ministers successfully reconcile their Christianity with a belief in restricting their own congregations by more or less direct methods. Injustice towards the Negro in the courts and by the police has become more subtle, to avoid sudden descents of Federal investigators, but none the less exists.

While the law has integrated all public facilities—restaurants and cinemas, etc.—the law can do nothing about economic realities : it is very rare to see a Negro in a white restaurant, because he cannot afford to eat there. There are not many restaurants in the towns which would dare to refuse a Negro service (many more do in the country where it is easier to escape attention for discrimination), because in the towns the Negro communities are sufficiently well-organised to be able to make trouble. But again, there are endless subtler ways of making it clear that a customer is unwelcome.

The business of school segregation is made easier by the residential segregation. In the North, some cities have overcome this by sending ghetto children by bus to areas where they can attend white schools, to break the de facto segregation. But in the South, where the will to do this does not exist, it is hard to compel city school boards to do it.

What is most depressing, however, is that as in many parts of the South, even the more prominent members of the Negro community seem to have run out of steam in the battle to keep change moving. The slower tempo of life in the South obviously affects Negroes as well as whites. The Civil Rights movement has tended to move by stops and starts rather than by steady progression. It is not that some of the Negro leaders I talked to in Montgomery seemed to lack the desire for change—they hasten to explain how difficult the situation remains. They just didn't seem to be doing much about it. This is no special criticism of the men living and working in such an atmosphere. It is just a statement of fact.

As I was in Montgomery a few weeks before the death of Lurleen Wallace, George Wallace was then still the effective master of Alabama. Indeed the story is told of Lurleen Wallace, soon after her election, coming into the state-house one morning and asking: "Where's the Governor?" She was almost surprised to be reminded: "You *are* the Governor!"

It's surprisingly difficult to hate George Wallace, dealing with him in the flesh. Another small man, physically, with a cocky, aggressive, earnest manner that somehow adds up to a demagogue of outstanding ability. The sheer speed of his remarks and answers enables him to fire across a string of untruths in such a way as to escape unquestioned until minutes, even hours later. He works hard at being liked, whatever his public manner: his remarks to journalists, especially foreign ones, are usually couched in a pathetically petulant style, with the unspoken defiance hanging on the end of every sentence.

Like so many white segregationists, his arguments are based on the "freedom of choice" ideal. That is to say, he considers that no one should have to be part of an integrated school, hospital or society if they do not want to. It is impossible to conduct a very rational argument about the flaw in this reasoning—that if whites are allowed to choose whether they should be integrated or not, why should the Negroes not be allowed to choose whether they are segregated?—because the issue becomes clouded in bombast about the importance of preserving law and order, keeping the Federal Government out of states' affairs and not giving foreign aid to countries which refuse to toe the political line.

Wallace bustles around his offices followed by his team of aides (who last May were dutifully spreading the word that if anyone wanted to see Wallace after 1968, they could look for him in the White House), proudest of all, perhaps, of being an "honest man".

"Up North," he says, "they to and fro all the time about Negroes and riots and what should be done and what shouldn't. All the time, they really think the same as we do, it's just that we're the only ones not afraid to say it."

There is an unpleasant degree of truth lurking there somewhere. Hodding Carter, a white liberal journalist in the South, sees in the attitude of the white middle classes in the Northern cities looking at the ghetto Negroes "a population watching with the fascinated horror of a chicken waiting for a coiled snake to strike". There seems little trace of any such fear among white Southerners. Anger, yes, at the manner in which laws have been thrust upon them, compelling change : but no great apprehension. One Colonel in charge of finding army draftees in Alabama calls himself the "coon-trapper". The major national television broadcasts emanating from New York and Washington are regarded with bitter hatred for their coverage of the South. Traditional Southern hospitality gives noticeably at the seams if a visitor is found to have "interfering" opinions. But there is a faith that it will all be right in the end, that the demon change will be kept at bay, which one suspects many white Northerners would be glad to possess.

Driving from Montgomery, Alabama, to Jackson, Mississippi, one sees the land change yet again. In Georgia, there is the dark red earth and the deep green woods stretching for miles upon miles. As one moves across Alabama, sandier ground turns into the darker soil of the flatlands which are universal in Mississippi. It is a wonderful region visually, if you can ignore the occasional roadside poster demanding : "Impeach Earl Warren", and if you do not attach too much significance to the fact that there are always many Negroes to be seen walking along the roads—very rarely a white man. Always there are the porches with the quiet figures who seem to sit on them all day long—because there is nothing else to do. Stopping at a restaurant on the road, a friend was unwise enough to antagonise the counter girl by discussing Alabama loudly and unfavourably. But when we left, she still came out with the traditional Southern pleasantry : "Come back and see us all!" This time it sounded so insincere that he glanced back : "You didn't really mean that, did you?" "Ah didn't say *when*," she spat back. . . .

Jackson, Mississippi, is an unprepossessing place—like so many Southern towns, it has the neon and squalor of Northern city centres without the corresponding facilities and advantages. Its TV and radio stations had achieved a certain notoriety some time before, when a civil rights group brought a brief before the Federal Communications Commission demanding that their licences not be renewed, on the grounds that they were not fulfilling any function as a public service. Like so many other Southern TV stations, they rigidly refrained from screening any documentaries or news material put out by the national networks that had any bearing on local issues of hunger, race or poverty. The stations now comply with the minimum requirements of the law in this respect, but their character is not dissimilar from that of many newspapers in the region, which still have separate white and Negro social pages.

But the tragedy of Mississippi lies some two hours drive from Jackson, in the heart of the Mississippi Delta which contains some of the richest farm land in America. The advent of national minimum wage laws began to hasten the inevitable, and make even those Negroes who had made a little money by casual labour completely redundant. In the Delta, sixty-three per cent of the population live below the national poverty level, and of those a significant number are actually starving. There are only about 30,000 industrial jobs available in the entire area, while there are hundreds of thousands of Negroes in desperate need of new work. Most of all, those who have been deprived of proper care, food and education* at an early age, have already lost their battle with life : they can never properly catch up.

"The first five years are the vital ones," a civil rights worker told me. "If they can't be helped then, it's too late. That means that in these last five years, we've lost another whole generation. . . ."

In the midst of the desolation, a number of small organisations work against all the odds to see what can be built up and saved. They are the new missionaries with a task the old brand would not envy. The Delta Ministry is probably the most famous —hated by the Mississippi whites, deriving a good deal of its finance, ironically, from foreign churches, staffed by a handful of men and women who must live among the Negro community whether they like it or not, because the white will have nothing to do with them. One girl I met from Iowa had already spent a year there, earning 2,000 dollars a year, living in conditions no better than those she and her colleagues are trying to improve, but perfectly happy : "How does one manage on that kind of money? One just learns to do without. . . ."

Voter registration is one of the key tasks—persuading Negroes to play a role in the political structure, because if enough of them vote, it is possible in some areas to gain political control in the end, and thus, more important, fiscal control. "But there are still some Negroes in Mississippi who really don't know that they're even allowed to vote," I was told. Vocational training schemes have been set up : one permanent base at which

* There is no compulsory education in Mississippi.

unskilled and underfed families can come to live while they learn new trades is known as Freedom City. Freedom City is a cluster of shacks—it seems a mockery of its name—but it is better than anything its occupants have known before. One reason for this is that there is nowhere near enough tax money in the area to finance new schools and facilities: the white tax assessors assess white landowners' property at a fraction of its worth. Many school districts and their controllers refuse to participate in the Federal programmes that are available to provide free lunches for underprivileged children. This stand is taken for the sacred cause of local autonomy—"Keep the 'Feds' out of here, whatever the cost". The struggle to break this attitude is slow and hard. Only three per cent of the Negroes in Mississippi are in white schools, fourteen years after the Supreme Court decreed desegregation! It is only a short time since many television newscasters were dissuaded from referring to Negroes as "niggers" on the air. In the towns, the white local authorities frequently do not enforce the housing codes on white landlords: thus, drainage and elementary facilities are often ignored. In Negro areas no one bothers to put up street lights.

On the streets of the Negro areas there is none of the aggressiveness or belligerence of those in the North. Old men and young men in their blue overalls move with the air of having nowhere special to go. When they glance at a strange white man passing by, it is with only vaguely-focused curiosity, not the hard defiant stare of Detroit or Chicago. The old-age pension is around fifty dollars a month, and welfare payments have on occasion been withdrawn without explanation from those who demonstrated for increases outside the State Capitol.

"We don't believe in revolution à la Carmichael down here," said Sue, the white civil rights worker. "It'd be genocide if the whites thought a serious attempt was being made—in fact that's why we'd be so scared if there was a riot." She works in the Delta "because I think it's the only place in America where the church is trying to do what it should".

Poverty and hunger, hunger and poverty: at the last census in 1960, it was found that the median annual income of Negroes —before welfare payments or other aid—was 465 dollars. Eight years ago, it was estimated that there were more than 60,000 Negroes employed in handpicking cotton in the Delta. There are now estimated to be less than 2,000. Estimates for current unemployment figures are around 100,000 for the area. Most of these are black.

If the Delta is justly famous as a symbol of America's worst, there are so many places far from it where injustice and misery thrive. Often, the whites continue to ignore or even perpetuate the problems. The Mayor of Jackson, Mississippi, declared one day with pride : "There are no slums in Jackson !" He was persuaded to take a tour of his own city, after which he admitted that he must completely recant his earlier statement. In some places, integration has moved successfully because shopowners have realised that integration can be "good for business". But there is still much de facto segregation in cinemas. It is generally true that the Ku Klux Klan is an organisation which nowadays makes more noise than serious trouble. But in Laurel, Mississippi, attempts to integrate an industrial plant in the interests of expansion were followed by a year of violence, destruction, fire bombings and at least one death—all of this undisguisedly inspired by the Klan. The plant is now working again, but at a lower capacity than before the start of its expansion plan. New housing schemes in many places are mere gestures; it is not uncommon to find that housing built for tenants with large families have only two bedrooms. Corruption is rife in many of the Federal programmes being administered by local authorities.

In the midst of it all, the Negro church ministers, almost invariably the leaders of their communities, hold their brethren together in the cause of civil rights. The emphasis at local meetings of the National Association for the Advancement of Coloured People is often in sharp contrast with similar gatherings in the North : unity is all important, whereas in the North fragmentation of interest and opinion is accepted as not only inevitable but even desirable.

On a Sunday afternoon perhaps sixty or seventy Negroes, mostly middle-aged, almost all with their wives (although the wives will probably sit as a group on their own) will gather in the choking heat of some small church to hear the minister reminding them : "All the Negro in America seeks is a chance to prove what he can do. . . ." The audience will chant "Yeeeaah" at almost every sentence in a quiet monotone, the minister constantly mops his brow in the sweaty atmosphere. There is no air of excitement—just attention. The goals these men seek are far more modest than those of the ghettoes. They are ordered and orderly, courteous and friendly, interested and curious; but they do not seem to have the anger in their hearts that one finds in the North. They are thankful for what little they have.

"Until three or four years ago, the Southern Negro had more patience, more faith in the white man than his Northern counterpart," I was told by an expert at the Southern Regional Council, who have done more than anyone to tell America what is going on in the South through reports, studies and statistical surveys—and are cordially hated by the white Southerners for their pains.

"Now, this is changing, and I think Southern Negroes are becoming more like those in the North—disillusioned and cynical. What has supported them for so long is the tangible progress made. They have appreciated what has been accomplished in their lifetimes in changing the law. But now they see that changing the law does not seem to have made as much difference as they hoped in day-to-day life. They ask: 'What can we do now, when all the laws are changed and much is still wrong?' I thought after Martin Luther King was murdered that in some ways there was a better chance than ever before for Negroes and whites to work together. But now I'm not so sure. It's very difficult to escape the fact that whereas before, we could get some money from the North to keep things moving down here, they're now using everything they can lay their hands on up there to save their own necks."

Yet on the day Martin Luther King was shot in Memphis, the South was quiet. Someone neatly summarised the attitude of the Negro in the ghetto for me as "If we can't eat off the table, we'll kick the ****ing legs off it!" It seems very dangerous if America is to forget once again that in the South the table is even more rickety than in the Northern cities.

REQUIEM : THE POOR PEOPLE'S MARCH ON WASHINGTON

It is impossible to turn away from any study of the racial situation in America without taking at least a glance at an event which occupied much of the nation's attention during May and June, 1968 : the Poor People's March on Washington.

The March had been conceived by Martin Luther King before his death. It was intended to draw attention in the most dramatic manner to the plight of the poor in America, and after King was assassinated, it was quickly decided that the March should go ahead as planned, but under the direction of the Reverend Ralph Abernathy, King's successor as head of the Southern Christian Leadership Conference. Even now, months after the event, no one is certain whether the March was merely a useful continuation of King's strategy of non-violent protest, or the swan-song of the great movement which had dominated civil rights in the 1950s.

The Southern Christian Leadership Conference was probably the strongest civil rights organisation in America under Martin Luther King. Based in Atlanta, Georgia, it brought together groups of varied interest and opinion under King's leadership, elements which may never be so united again. Its influence extended far beyond the South from whence it sprang, although it was never as well organised in the North where its religious strength made less impact.

The Reverend Abernathy was King's most loyal subordinate, and it was largely in recognition of this that King is thought to have nominated Abernathy to succeed him in the event of any mishap befalling King. After the assassination, when Abernathy had recovered from the shock which seemed to numb him for several days, he set about organising the Poor People's March with more noise than sound logistics. He talked a great deal about visions from above, about his closeness to "Martin" in death as well as life, about his own role as Joshua leading his people to the promised land. It was not that this made him sound arrogant—it was that he seemed as much concerned with persuading himself that this was all so as with convincing his followers. He appeared to lack self-confidence as well as organising ability. Some observers argue that the whites who criticise Abernathy do so because they do not understand him, and while King was comprehensible to the white power structure with his education and background, Abernathy, a man of humbler learning, is in closer touch with his own people. This is not altogether convincing. In the battles within the SCLC since King's death, there has been no sign that Abernathy can command the loyalty of his own followers any more than the respect of the white establishment.

The prospect of the Poor People's March reduced Washington to both fury and fright. Abernathy announced that the marchers would converge from all over the country on the capital, and there encamp themselves for as long as it took to get really effective action against poverty from the Administration. Members of Congress urged that the marchers should be forbidden to camp. Local citizens foresaw a blood-bath once the deprived were gathered in thousands on their doorsteps. Not only the local citizens, either. Washington is normally a major tourist centre during the summer, but the combination of the April riots and the Poor People's March drastically reduced the number of visitors.

Nevertheless, a camping permit was issued, and an encampment of shacks was created in the Washington Mall park. At the beginning of May, Abernathy's legions were on the move and starting to trickle into the city—their entrance often delayed because of unprepared accommodation. Progress of the various sections of the March across America was peaceful and relatively speedy—the marchers only walked part of the way and took buses the rest. There were a number of incidents in the South—one that could have been serious in Mississippi, where the police acted with determined brutality. But somehow, even such potentially threatening moments as marchers finding themselves in Montgomery on the same day as Lurleen Wallace's funeral were overcome quietly, and the convoys converged on Washington.

Thus far, it seemed, it was only the organisation that had failed: huts being built too slowly, convoys in the wrong places at the wrong times, the administration of Resurrection City, as the encampment became called, being shifted from hand to hand in SCLC in-fighting. But during the last weeks of May and the first of June, more drastic holes appeared in the entire plan. First, many of the genuine poor, who had left their homes to bring their families from the South to seek hope, found misery worse in Resurrection City than in their normal lives : the weather alternately turned the site into a muddy morass and a baking desert. Petty crime and internal disorder became frequent. Squabbles between the Negroes, whites, Indians and Mexicans worsened in the confined atmosphere. Many went home, deeply disappointed. Abernathy endeavoured to shrug off the mass desertions, without conviction.

More serious than this, however, was the complete disarray regarding the aims of the March. The Administration appeared genuinely anxious to do everything possible to meet the Marchers' demands. Abernathy and his colleagues proved incapable of coming up with any faintly practical schemes on which the Government might be asked to act. The March leaders would make appointments to see senior Cabinet officers and then fail to turn up. Such demonstrations as took place were fragmented and apparently unorganised. And as the life of Resurrection City became the subject of closer and closer press scrutiny—and the papers had hitherto bent backwards to be helpful—new facts became clear : the number of America's genuine poor represented on the March declined as more and more went home. The campaign seemed dominated by a collection of white hippies, young Negroes from the city gangs and plain hoodlums of all kinds and colours. I had myself covered the western leg of the March on its way through Kentucky, and had been deeply depressed by the contrast between those present and the grindingly poor of the Mississippi Delta, from whence I had only recently come. Mexicans smoking marijuana in an alley outside the hall where the marchers were spending the night : whisky and beer flowing freely, marchers declining the free food provided to buy their own at drugstores, expense no object : it all seemed such a far cry from America's poor. I asked one young white from the University of California why he was on the March. "Well, I'm poor, aren't I?" He laughed. "Why am I poor? Oh, I'm poor voluntarily." Operations seemed to be largely controlled by Negro youths from Los Angeles, who were far more frightening than any group I'd met in the ghettoes. In that one convoy of perhaps six hundred people, there seemed more representatives of the dregs of the nation than of the under-privileged. The tragedy was that for so many Americans who have not seen Appalachia, the Delta, or the other areas of their country where there is real hardship, these marchers were representative of the poor they were being asked to help. Parsimonious towards welfare programmes already, they were not only unimpressed but angry.

In Resurrection City by early June, there had been a series of increasingly unpleasant incidents involving marchers. A Negro journalist walking near the compound was seriously beaten up and had his walkie-talkie radio stolen by young marchers. The marshals originally chosen to police the camp, had to be replaced by older men, because their predecessors proved to cause more trouble than they prevented. Throughout it all, Abernathy and his men kept assuring the world in increasingly petulant tones that nothing was wrong. Then came the day when criticism of the SCLC leaders became almost universal. Despairing of their vagueness, Bayard Rustin, one of the older and most successful civil rights organisers who had been called in to plan a great rally for the March, issued a highly practical, reasonable, precise list of demands as the March's formal aims. The Government gave a sigh of relief, the demands were greeted generally as refreshingly reasonable and down to earth. Not so for Abernathy and the SCLC leadership, who felt that their grip was already in danger. They announced that Rustin had been unauthorised to speak for the March and, after more in-fighting, that he had withdrawn from organising the rally. One of his conditions for involvement in the March was that there should be some clearly established and tangible goals for it. These were not found, so he went.

When the great rally eventually took place on June 19th, it received wide and relieved comment, mostly because Washington seemed surprised that nothing actively disastrous took place. The subsequent incarceration of Abernathy for illegal demonstrating (not connected with the actual rally) caused no surprise. It had been widely suggested that he would deliberately aim for a short jail sentence as a means of retrieving some of his own badly dented prestige. After further worried negotiating by the

Government, afraid they would never get rid of Resurrection City, those few marchers who had not already left were forcibly evicted and the site was closed down—its permit having expired after several renewals. By the time it was bulldozed away, the squalor and shambles far surpassed the worst of the Mississippi Delta.

The Reverend Abernathy, it was felt before the March, would make or break his reputation with it. It now looks very much as if he broke it. That is not necessarily to suggest that he will suddenly and dramatically be deposed as head of SCLC (although that too is possible). More likely, he will be gradually edged aside. It has even been suggested that Mrs. Coretta King, Martin Luther King's widow, may play an increasingly prominent role in the organisation. Beyond this, it is likely that the civil rights movement will become more fragmented than ever since the March. Vast sums of money were donated to SCLC after King's assassination, much of which was spent in the March. But even now, there may be enough left to maintain SCLC's currently waning influence for somewhat longer. There are others behind Abernathy—notably Andrew Young, another former King aide—who have the organising ability and strategic planning talents to hold the SCLC together, providing a "front man" of sufficiently charismatic personality is in charge.

But there is no doubt that the Poor People's March destroyed much of the national goodwill towards the civil rights movement that existed after King's assassination. Whether the March correspondingly produced any real results to the benefit of the poor seems highly doubtful. The Administration, anxious to "show willing", expedited some of the food programmes already in existence. But Congress was taken more by anger than by sympathy for the strange assortment of protesters who dominated Washington's city life for several weeks.

Covering the Poor People's March, I felt it was as tragic an event as any in 1968. From a conception of a great idea which might, just might, have worked in other hands, there appeared a picture of chaotic and aimless squalor dominated by some of the least attractive personalities I saw in America during the year. For this, it is hard to blame the Reverend Abernathy, very obviously a decent and sincere man hopelessly out of his depth as a leader of such a movement. But if non-violent and peaceful progress towards racial justice in America is to be made, leaders of far greater personal quality and strength of purpose must emerge, and emerge quickly. Martin Luther King himself was finding it hard to maintain the momentum of his plans during the last months of his life; a respect for his memory alone will not be enough to keep the civil rights movement civil.

America in 1968 suffered an incredible series of sudden disasters which monopolised newspapers and television channels for days on end, and which brought a deep and immediate agony to the nation. But behind the assassinations and urban riots, the political crises and upheavals, perhaps nothing disturbed America more profoundly than the apparent alienation of her youth. Issues and incidents became increasingly interwoven: the political successes of Senator Eugene McCarthy and the activities of the students who did so much to put him in the fore; the tragedy of the Vietnam war and the draft protesters who so publicly declined to regard it as their battle; the ever-increasing evidence of a generation gap which more and more Americans were finding in their own homes. All these things made the universities increasingly focal points of very worried attention. To many Americans, it seemed bad enough that the Negro and the poor were waging war on their doorsteps, not to mention the Vietcong a few thousand miles away. . . .

In 1968, it appeared that it was not only the Communists and the underprivileged who were opposing the American Dream. It was their own children—the richest, best educated, most sophisticated children in the history of any society on earth.

CHAPTER 4

A NEW KIND OF BALL GAME

"If Senator Fulbright came here to speak, we could give the campus police the night off. But if a member of the Cabinet turned up, we'd have to call in the National Guard to keep the peace."

Malcolm Moos, President of the
University of Minnesota

IT SEEMS UNPROFITABLE to dwell in great detail on the chronology of one or more of the major university uprisings—and such they were—in America in recent months. There are, however, certain general characteristics which appear to emerge from a study of a series of incidents in 1967 and 1968.

The students were usually inspired in their actions by a compound of some or all of the following:

(1) Demands for a greater say in the running of the university, both in administration of their day-to-day personal lives and in directing academic programmes.

(2) Opposition to the Vietnam war, either voiced as a demonstration against the war in the abstract, or as a protest against military recruitment on the campus. The latter included objections to the recruitment of trainees for firms which make war material, most notably the Dow Chemical Corporation who manufacture napalm.

(3) Demands which related in some way or other to racial minorities. Perhaps requests for more scholarships for Negroes, or a drive by Negroes for campus courses in Negro culture, or a protest against some injustice against a racial minority perpetrated by the university authorities.

The most serious student revolt of the year took place at New York's Columbia University, and appeared to be inspired by a mixture of (1) and (3).* The immediate cause of the outbreaks of active dissention was the University plan for building a gymnasium on land adjacent to the Harlem Negro ghetto. It was suggested that the plan discriminated against Negroes in an area where more leisure facilities were badly needed for them. Students occupied several University buildings, and the ensuing battle lasted on and off for several weeks during May. A Negro militant group—not connected with the University—became involved, and conducted their own parallel but separate campaign within the University precincts. Peace was eventually restored on a very uneasy basis, more, it seemed, because of exhaustion on both sides than as a result of any tangible victories.

The battles at Columbia highlighted the attitudes and tactics which make up the background of most American university demonstrations, whatever their specific initial causes. The students' contempt for the university authorities ensured that any negotiations which took place need not be hindered by any superfluous respect for the senior faculty as such. Finding themselves in a quite unprecedented situation far beyond their experience, the senior faculty handled it in a manner which appeared to justify their charges' contempt. And the police, when summoned to evict the students from the buildings they had occupied, displayed a ruthlessness which repaid in full the students' obvious loathing for them.

Abe Fortas, Chief Justice designate of the Supreme Court, produced a fascinating pamphlet shortly before his appointment,† outlining his view of the rights of public dissent under the American Constitution. His key point in relation to civil disobedience was that it is essential for anyone who decides on this course of action to draw attention to his grievances, to accept the consequences of his act. In other words, if you commit an act of trespass under the law by holding a sit-down demonstration, you must then accept that under the law you will be removed and taken for trial : "This is civil disobedience in the classic tradition". Some American dissenters, youthful and otherwise, have accepted this principle when arrested or carried away for obstructing entrances to draft induction centres,

* This massive revolt was sparked by one further demand: that the University sever its connection with the Institute for Defence Analyses, a civilian research arm of the Pentagon.

† Never finally confirmed by the Senate, Fortas withdrew.

etc. But it has become increasingly characteristic of student demonstrations and protests that the participants, when the moment of truth comes, are sufficiently roused to ignore the law and stand and fight, be their opponents other students, campus police or civil police. The issue in these cases is often further complicated by questions relating to the law within university precincts: how valid is it, for example, for university authorities to accuse students blockading one of the university buildings of trespass in order to secure their ejection?

All these fine points relating to students, universities and the law might seem irrelevant but for the students' increasing use of the law as a means of pressing their grievances or redressing past wrongs. It is still a hotly argued issue whether students should be permitted to be represented by counsel when facing university authorities, although many campuses have already given way on this point. Universities are sharply divided as to the desirability of calling in the police to deal with internal students' revolts—largely because to do so invariably appears to cause outbreaks of violence even if these have not already taken place. The practice of taking hostages to be held during the course of a siege has also been on the increase, further intensifying pressure to bring in the law. Even beyond that, given the necessity of summoning police help—should they then be permitted to use the disabling and supposedly harmless chemical Mace spray to subdue the rebels? These are the sort of problems which must be argued at many university faculty meetings or, worse, in the heat of some sudden outbreak of student unrest.

American university revolts appear to differ from those in England largely in their intensity. It may be because at English universities students retain some respect for the authorities by virtue of their office, if not their persons. The struggle in England does not yet seem to have become a simple matter of "us" as against "them", especially where the police are concerned.

Finally, the most striking quality about the American student revolts is the vagueness which usually surrounds the question of what the students really want. Their published demands are often so patently unreasonable as to be obviously inacceptable—even to their proponents. And when negotiations between authorities and students eventually take place, the main point at issue usually seems to become whether those involved should be punished for crimes committed during the protest, rather than what should be done to remedy the original grievances.

It is important to add in this context that none of the foregoing should suggest that American students have nothing to complain about. Rather, it is intended as an illustration of the depressing complexity of the situation. Like so much else in America of 1968, it leaves one sadly bewildered rather than especially committed to any one cause.

*   *   *

Such has been the success of the American ideal of offering an opportunity of higher education to every child of school-leaving age that something like forty-five per cent of them now go on to some kind of university or technical training (although the percentage of Negroes is considerably lower). University education in America is financed in a wide variety of ways, and it is a matter of personal opinion whether one considers that all of them help in creating the kind of environment a university needs.

Some students are wholly financed from their parents' income. Others are paid for entirely, or in part, by grants from state, college, university, or in some cases private foundations of one kind or another. The tradition of university financing is such that many students when they begin their courses have little idea or worry how they will be paying for the end of them. It is common to stop halfway from choice or necessity and then come back later to complete the degree. There are many students who combine university work with a job, either for pocket money or to help pay the fees, and a number who manage to graduate—perhaps with intermittent stops and starts —financed entirely by their own efforts. A very large number indeed take jobs in vacations, perhaps not specially from necessity but because it is an accepted convention to do so, and because the American economy has no difficulty in accommodating students in relatively high-paying holiday jobs.

All this helps to create the often very fragmented atmosphere on American campuses, sometimes only noticeable in small ways, such as students who disappear after lunch every day because they earn a little money by doing the washing-up in the dining rooms, and sometimes more obviously, in the wide variety of age groups at any given university, and in the differing patterns of living and study. The latter, of course, is accentuated by the growing necessity of having far more than a mere Bachelor's degree to find a good job. It's not uncommon to stay for years at a university doing post-graduate research, not only as an end in itself, but as a necessary stepping-stone to higher things. Once again, the difference from the situation in an English university may only be relative—the structure is the same. But at most English universities, the graduate student remains a side show, if only because of his smaller numbers, while in America the converse is becoming increasingly the case.

Because American society appreciated it faster than any other in the world, and had the money to exploit it, the vast expansion of the industry of knowledge in the last few years has made American universities almost as significant as the corporate giants in national planning. The libraries, the scientific facilities, the congregation of talent have multiplied each other over the years until many small colleges have been squeezed out because, like so much else in the twentieth century, they have simply failed to meet the minimum practicable standards of size.

Thus American higher education is dominated by a university complex in which there may be 40,000 students within a single administrative structure. The universities of California, Michigan, Minnesota and the others like them boast a faculty list many of whose members are top government and industrial advisers. But this in itself creates a dubious situation. The universities argue that to have national figures on the teaching staff lends a sense of immediacy and relevance to the students' education which is highly beneficial. But then again, it seems questionable how much personal communication is possible between students and a professor who spends half the week in Washington and the other half dashing between classrooms and the hot line to publishers, business or government. Many junior faculty members are already exasperated by the emphasis placed on the importance of their completing a book as speedily as possible after joining a university. And in the light of present experience at American universities, the argument of the president who told me he thought it better that a great teacher should be heard for half an hour by 1,000 students on closed circuit TV rather than for ten hours by twenty students at a personal seminar seems distinctly unconvincing. More specifically, it would not seem to matter much if most professors a student sees are only at a distance, so long as he becomes personally familiar with some of the others. But the pressure of numbers alone seems to dictate more and more that personal contacts are minimal. This again may contribute to the lack of any great affection for their alma mater on the part of many students.

Talking to a senior planner at the University of Michigan at Ann Arbor, it appeared that it wasn't so much money or talent that was lacking. "It's just," he said "that I sometimes feel I might as well have been called in to create some huge factory."

Somewhere in the pipeline of the university hierarchy, and it is not easy to discover exactly where, a faith in prestige of a rather unintellectual character seems to have become inculcated: there often appears to be a striving to have the *biggest* or the *most* of something regardless of where this fits in with the educational concept. Ambitions to create brilliant football or basketball teams, even if you have to give scholarships to morons who will then become professional athletes for the duration of their stay at the university, have been common for very many years. But it is less easy to understand why the creation of a gigantic modern concert hall should be sought less for its functional potential than for the opportunity to hire an architect of national stature to create an outstanding example of modern building: this especially on campuses where faculty members are already seriously overworked, and cash is badly needed to recruit more teachers.

Perhaps it all becomes much more easily comprehensible if one accepts the view of modern American state universities as power structures in their own right, which indeed one must. I may be accused of laying too much emphasis on the educational giants (giants in quantity if not quality, that is). But so much of the headline-making news and so many trends in student thinking start on their campuses that one inevitably looks at them with special curiosity. The snowball which eventually hits a small-town college in Wisconsin has almost inevitably started with a student protest at the big state university in Madison.

Many American state universities are what are termed "land grant" universities. That is to say, they were originally established on land granted by the state in which they are situated, and remain to this day under the indirect control of that state's legislature. The original brief from the legislature to the university authorities usually included some more or less direct instruction to educate the state's sons to be useful members of the society. And it's just this role that many American universities still see themselves as playing : they are trying to turn out a graduate who will be of some value both to himself and to the social structure to which he is supposed to belong. One of the most interesting questions that has emerged from student unrest in recent months and years, and one that the students themselves often seem unable to answer articulately is : to what extent is student disenchantment with the universities provoked by unwillingness to accept this principle of being educated for some clearly grooved, well-defined end? One of the best and funniest American films of 1967 was entitled *The Graduate,* and concerned a young man who, having succeeded brilliantly at university, resisted the idea of following a path that then seemed so soundly organised for him. Are American universities placing enough emphasis, or any emphasis at all for that matter, on education for education's sake? They certainly appear to have carried the theory of specialist training to its logical conclusion. Professionalism has always been a classic American virtue, but the question now seems to arise whether in the drive for professionalism, the universities, specialising for specialising's sake, are trying to teach some skills which are almost unteachable. At the risk of being parochial, one might cite the journalism schools which are now so much a part of many US campuses. Students majoring in journalism appear to have been imbued with the idea that it's a skill which can be taught, like brick-laying. Perhaps one of the reasons this rationale has become necessary is that there are such wide differences in the abilities of students taking any given course, since entrance qualifications for the universities are seldom very rigorous.

Regardless of how hard many American students work once at a university, or of their varying attitudes to being groomed on production-line methods, today they inevitably have self-confidence of a kind unknown to the young anywhere in the world before the war. All of us, and young Americans especially, form the first sizeable generation in history who *know*, and have known from birth, that there is not the slightest chance that we shall starve, whether or not we fail in our chosen careers. This is one of the reasons why it's often difficult to understand the surprise that is expressed at student activism, good or bad. The simple fact that we don't have the more basic and more frighteningly personal fears of our parents' generation ensures that unless we become complete vegetables, we shall have more time and more opportunity to make our presence felt—for better or for worse. This seems forseeable, although so often when American papers report some new outbreak of student demonstrations or youthful revolt, there is a note of vague surprise in the background. Before considering America's fears and problems with her students and her youth, one must have accepted these two considerations: firstly, as outlined above, the situation prevailing within the great universities; secondly, and probably more important, the inevitability of activism of some kind—the question only relating precisely to what and why. The last point, if anything, makes the current student revolt seem much less frightening than many Americans appear prepared to accept. One of 1968's stranger American films, *Wild in the Streets,* concerned the imagined take-over of the country by the young, one of whom becomes President, with dire consequences. In one scene, a senator appeals to the boy's mother, saying that her son's actions are paralysing the country. "Senator," replies the mother determinedly, "if my son is paralysing the country, I am sure he has a very good reason for paralysing the country!" In the context of 1968, that remark could much more appropriately have been made by almost any American student. It's the absolute conviction that the ends justify the means that is changing the face of youthful protest, not the nature of what is being said; and violent protest by the young only seems such an alarming phenomenon because human memory is too short to remember a few decades back to the last of such outbursts.

Even having said all this, it is essential to remember just how small the number of hard-core student activists really is. Perhaps the most practical link one can find between them and their idol, the Cuban revolutionary, Che Guevara, is the influence they have successfully wielded as a minority employing the campus equivalent of guerilla tactics. It's not only that within any given university the numbers of those engaged in active combat are limited; it's that disturbances usually take place within the precincts of a recurring handful of universites. On many small college campuses across the country, there are less articulate and less forceful groups with the same general ambitions and feelings. But it's very rarely that they are willing to nail their flag to the mast, if to do so will bring about an open breach with the authorities. This may be partly due to the fact that their relationship towards the college as an entity and towards the faculty is a much more personal one, which of course operates both ways, in that the faculty can and does exercise a more direct influence on its charges. Similarly, a small college or university student meets far fewer of the conflicting social and political pressures that play so large a role at the big state universities. And since universities nowadays may have as much a reputation for their activism as for their educational facilities, I have met numbers of students who have chosen to go to, say, Berkeley, because there they know they will be able to get involved in political activity on the widest scale available. I heard one girl at Berkeley express her disenchantment on getting there and finding that the campus actually had a football team—"like anywhere else . . ."

University protest concerning internal affairs usually revolve around two more or less separate issues : what degree of control should the students be permitted to exercise over their own personal lives? And secondly, and a much more sensitive issue, to what extent should students be permitted to control or even advise on academic affairs? On the first point, most of the big universities are rapidly giving way. It is being acknowledged that every girl in the universities of 1968 has the right to get pregnant if she wants to. And such institutions as limited visiting hours between men's and girls' halls are being abolished in favour of more relaxed arrangements. Most of the pressure to retain the university's control on students' personal lives comes, according to one president I talked to, from their parents.

"In anything relating to their personal affairs," he said, "we will give them anything they want within reason. What we will not do under any circumstances, however, is to permit students to exercise control over the appointments and careers of faculty members."

This enters the second area of student-university disagreement, and is one on which at present both sides appear deadlocked. Once again, it's worth remembering that many university students show no signs of particularly wanting a say in whether their professor gets a salary raise or not. But those activists who have demanded a greater role in planning their own academic courses often link to this requests for student participation in deciding who teaches them. Some of the more liberal authorities agree that the students' advice or opinions should be both sought and heard. But nowhere does there seem any sign that any university is prepared to accept student opinion as binding in matters academic. This is likely to remain a sensitive area for a long time to come.

If students are dissatisfied at a personal level with the structure and aims of their universities, however, how much more do they seem disenchanted with the wider aims of the whole society into which they have been thrust. The rise of Eugene McCarthy and the fantastic appeal of his message to the students and the young in general is a story that belongs later on, but it's undisputed that a very large number of American students more or less actively oppose the Vietnam war. Many more again are deeply disturbed by the situation of the racial minorities within the country, although often they're both ill-informed and inarticulate when asked to come down to practicalities. The war is easier to oppose, because the issue there has become to many the simple one of "stay in" or "get out". Even here, it's often surprising how little student leaders seem to know about the facts of the Vietnam situation when being cross-questioned.

What seems much more significant is that in their rejection of the values of flag and country, which means so much to their parents, there are emerging three distinct paths for young Americans to follow : either they become passionately concerned to change their society, and become activists of one kind or another both on and off their campus; or, although dissatisfied with society, they make themselves fit into it by graduating in the conventional manner and moving on to a conventional job in the family pattern (this obviously accounts for much the highest percentage); or, lacking the inclination for working towards change and the enthusiasm for a role in society as it is, they drop out altogether.

A lot has been written and said about the hippies of San Francisco and elsewhere, even now, when they are dying—if they ever really lived. Although the hippies were a fascinating temporary phenomenon, most of the members of the third group of students which I've just mentioned, are not in the slightest degree interested in the cult of love and flowers or anything else. They're only concerned with leading the most enjoyable possible lives with the least possible effort. They are, in other words, hedonists. They work as and when they have to, to make enough money to survive (in America it's remarkable how well you can do working part-time with a reasonable education and the right—or wrong—kind of friends). California is their happy hunting ground, because California happens to have an agreeable climate and enough surplus resources to sustain significant numbers of parasites. Their ranks may include students, drop-outs from university, those who did not go to university at all, and perhaps a few graduates. They could not exist except in a society with enormous personal and parental resources, and their numbers seem bound to increase as these resources become more and more readily available. If the American parent persists in his concern for his children's stability and reasonableness, he might worry a bit less about those who battle with the police in university demonstrations, and a bit more about those who are doing absolutely nothing.

I lived in an apartment building just off Sunset Boulevard in Los Angeles for a month. The other tenants in the block were aged between twenty and thirty, apparently largely unemployed, and evidently very well off financially. Illegal blackjack games sometimes lasted for thirty-six hours at a stretch, with anything up to $500 changing hands. One or two flats in the block usually served as the centre for communal activity, and in these by late evening there might be ten or fifteen people playing cards, watching TV, or rather indifferently making love in one of the bedrooms with any girl they had managed to pick up on the Sunset Strip. As the building had a swimming pool, this was usually the focal point during the day, while the girls who drifted in and out at irregular intervals earned their keep cleaning up after a fashion. Deliveries of boxes of fried chicken or pizza took care of feeding problems, and coca-cola and whisky disappeared in about equal quantities. Every few days, somebody or other would disappear briefly to do a little work : one girl worked as a stripper, another man as a night-club agent. Someone else put in a few hours a week in a drugstore, and yet another sold secondhand cars—almost everyone in the building seemed to have some kind of car, heaven knows how.

The girls seemed the saddest, because their permanence or otherwise was determined by the rather arbitrary moods of whoever was keeping them. One was kept busy flying to Philadelphia once a fortnight to report to a parole officer. Another, I remember, was complaining one night that the man with whom she lived didn't give her enough to eat. I asked her why she lived with him at all: "It's better than being a hooker, isn't it?" she replied. She was seventeen, had dropped out of school at fifteen, had a baby and been married by sixteen. Now, she had left the baby with her mother and come to Los Angeles for a slice of the easy life. The only jobs for which she seemed qualified were those that she considered beneath her, but she rejected them as being too badly paid. She wanted, she said, a nice house, a big car and a rich husband and she wasn't going to settle for anything less. To this end, she was prepared to put up with any hardship along the line—except actual work. She felt very sorry for herself.

It's easy to say that she doesn't sound deserving of much interest or sympathy. But such is the mobility of America today, and such is the disregard for living with one's parents unless one has some extraordinary affection for them, that the age of the young nomad has long since arrived. Girls seem even more prone to the life than men, and on any night in Hollywood, one can walk the boulevards and see strings of aimless teenyboppers hanging around outside the clubs, eager to make friends with anyone who will buy them a hamburger. Not only Hollywood : the same is true in most big cities. Begging has been a way of life for some time in hippy circles, and now in New York or on the West Coast it's a strange day when one can walk the streets without being asked at least two or three times for a dime, a quarter, a dollar or the fare to Long Island.

Returning once again to the apartment building in Los Angeles, perhaps the oddest feature of all was the contentment that seemed to prevail. No one seemed cursed by any great worries about the future, no one seemed anxious to look beyond tomorrow. Few of those living there had criminal records, and those that did were mostly on drug charges. Indeed, the building seemed to be raided at almost weekly intervals by police drug squads. In the middle of a blackjack game one night, a girl who had left the week before for San Francisco telephoned to ask if someone would drive up and bail her out on a drugs charge. Someone did.

It was certainly not that most of those living there had no chance of a reasonable, conventional career, if they wanted it. When politics or current events were being discussed, everyone seemed thoroughly aware of what was happening in the world; they all read the newspapers (some of the girls were possible exceptions); and apart from the customary taste for beards, moustaches, jeans and a dirty shirt as standard dress, it was one of the most conventionally friendly and hospitable little communities one could look for anywhere. It was simply that almost all those who were—and for all I know, still are—members of it, felt no interest at all in doing as their parents or even their contemporaries did, only in living the most pleasant as possible existence undisturbed by the world except the occasional vice squad detective (who might have been more usefully employed elsewhere anyway).

Once again, their way of life sparks the question of whose criteria are valid in assessing them? In the most obvious way, they don't harm anyone, perhaps not even themselves. But to the mainstream of American society, they are—like the hippies —evading responsibilities and declining to play a positive role in the maintenance of the structure which supports them. They themselves, incurious souls, are not especially concerned with the part the Founding Fathers played in making it possible for them to live as they do. They've merely sought and found a comfortable niche from which to watch the rest of the world rush by. No one as yet seems very certain whether their view will look as unclouded when they are twenty years older.

It may be argued that in looking at some of the young, both inside and outside American universities, one is taking too casual an attitude to a situation in which acts of virtual mutiny, and sometimes violence, have become a commonplace. But even ignoring the historical precedents, it seems equally justifiable to suggest that given the conservative character of American society in 1968, it is only determined action and protest that is noticed, far less acted upon. This is not an apology for the violent demonstration, any more than one can exist for the urban riots. It's simply a factor that makes student activism as difficult to condemn out of hand as civil disorders, and one that makes an observer less sympathetic than ever to the worried cries of American parents who seem convinced that their children are basely deserting both them and the values in which they believe.

America's problems, dilemmas, happinesses and sorrows in 1968 could be nowhere more accurately reflected than in the battle for the Democratic Party's Presidential nomination.

Partly this was because it seemed that only among the Democrats was there any real contest in which sides could be taken and feelings articulated. For while in the autumn of 1967 Governor Nelson Rockefeller of New York seemed a very serious contender for the Republican nomination, he dithered and procrastinated to such an extent in the early months of 1968 that he seemed determined to offer Richard Nixon a certain victory. He formally entered the race, then dropped out again and finally came back. He entered no primaries—and his write-in vote in such states as permit them was very small—and campaigned only spasmodically. To the acute disappointment of many Democrats who would have voted for Republican Rockefeller rather than Democrat Humphrey in the national election, he left all the initiatives to Nixon. The latter entered primaries unopposed to gain a vote of confidence from the Republicans, which he got. He campaigned vigorously on a platform which commanded some very solid support as the year went on with its crises and disasters: "fight fire with fire in the cities", he urged. "Law and order" was his slogan, with undertones of promises for tougher law courts, more police and no "surrender" in Vietnam. He was promising the mailed fist, if elected, to deal with America's disorders and unruliness. He seemed to an outsider the most depressing figure imaginable for a potential President. Put plainly, he looked untrustworthy, narrow-minded and self-righteous. But because his path to the Republican nomination looked clear, until after the conventions in August, he was a mere sideshow. The action was elsewhere.

Kennedy and McCarthy were two of the most fascinating political figures in recent American history. For a significant part of 1968, the stage was theirs. Perhaps Richard Nixon's only significant contribution to the year's election campaign was a jab he aimed at the Democrats during a spring speech:

"Eugene McCarthy is running for President; Robert Kennedy for King; and Hubert Humphrey for Foreman of the Ranch."

He had a point.

CHAPTER 5

A WAR ABOUT PEACE

"I run for the Presidency because I want the United
States to stand for the reconciliation of men. . . ."
Robert F. Kennedy—election poster, May, 1968

No two men, whether in the moments of high excitement
or awful tragedy, contributed more to the drama of the 1968
elections than Senators Robert F. Kennedy and Eugene
McCarthy. In some ways, this is rather peculiar, because it was
only at a few isolated moments during the campaign that either
seemed to have a real chance of securing the Democratic
Party's nomination as Presidential candidate.

Both Kennedy and McCarthy, on almost indistinguishable
platforms politically, were crying out for a new America, a
fresh look at old standards and values, a re-think of the policies
which have guided the country since the days of the frontier.
They opposed the Administration's handling of the Vietnam
war, and argued for a withdrawal of American forces as soon
and as best this could be achieved without being obliged to
undertake a humiliating Dunkirk. Both—Kennedy more obtru-
sively—sought action to change the conditions of the urban
ghettoes and stamp out poverty. They insisted that it was time
for new faces in government (Kennedy's might not be new, but
it at least looked young). They could truthfully add that if
Richard Nixon was elected President, it would be a mandate for
a defence of the status quo. And they tried to argue that even
with Lyndon Johnson out of the race, Hubert Humphrey still
represented an old and obsolete line of thought and style.

But when Robert Kennedy announced his own entry into
the race only days after the New Hampshire primary in March,
he seemed almost as much of a forlorn hope as Eugene
McCarthy. Then, when Lyndon Johnson announced his impending abdication, for a few short weeks Kennedy looked like
a front runner. But even as he was defeating McCarthy in the

Indiana and Nebraska primaries during early May, Hubert
Humphrey, not entered for either contest, was quietly gaining
convention delegates at a speed which made an ultimate
Kennedy victory at the convention seem almost impossible.
Because it was widely thought that if he could not win,
McCarthy would throw his support and his delegates to Hubert
Humphrey rather than Kennedy, when McCarthy beat
Kennedy in the Oregon primary at the beginning of June, the
die seemed cast. Kennedy couldn't win, not even by joining
forces with McCarthy (which he tried to induce the Minnesotan to do), nor could McCarthy. Hubert Humphrey, with the
tacit support of the Administration, was rallying support at
local party conventions in states which do not have primaries,
and looked already invincible. By the time Kennedy won the
California primary, his victory no longer seemed to matter.

While he and McCarthy had been commanding the headlines as they slogged out their Primary fight, the battle had
been fought and decided on the back pages, during Hubert's
quiet little trips around the country, ensuring that men who
would have backed Lyndon Johnson if he had run were now
committed to his deputy.

Even with Robert Kennedy's death, nothing seemed changed.
The fact of McCarthy's strong position in the national opinion
polls, of his solid bloc of Convention delegates, could not alter
the impressive lead of Hubert Humphrey. As the dates of the
national conventions and of the election itself drew near, in a
strange way they seemed completely anti-climactic. It was like
a Wimbledon in which all the best-loved seeds had been knocked
out in the first round—the finals were just plain depressing.

For what could compare with the spectacle of Eugene
McCarthy's "Children's Crusade" running rampant in the first
days of New Hampshire and Wisconsin? Or of Robert Kennedy
being greeted as he drove through the streets of the campaign
towns by a crowd and an adoration Clark Gable would have
envied? Although it was clear from early on that the real battle
for the Democratic nomination, if there was one, was between
Kennedy and Humphrey, the struggle that captured America's
imagination was between Kennedy and McCarthy. A television
debate between the two in the week before the California
primary finally confirmed what had always seemed the case:
that the two were ideologically almost indistinguishable. Ameri-

can elections revolve far more around personalities than around parties at any time, but in 1968 the political similarity between Kennedy and McCarthy ensured that the battle was a personal one. It really began on March 12th, New Hampshire day, and ended on June 5th, when Kennedy was shot in the hour of victory in the California primary.

* * *

"I'm Eugene McCarthy and I'm hoping you'll vote for me on March 12th." The shopper McCarthy had accosted in a New Hampshire supermarket looked him in the eye and ignored the proferred hand. "I'm a Republican and I shan't be voting for you." McCarthy, in a rapid undertone: "All right, but we'd better shake hands for the cameras". A rather grudging display of friendliness takes place, and McCarthy moves hastily on through the store, hotly pursued by a cavalcade of aides and newsmen. He corners voters hurriedly, exchanges a few words, leaves a pretty girl wearing a straw hat with a McCarthy band on it to hand out some pamphlets, and dashes on. He is not pleased by the effect his following convoy is having, trampling him every time he starts to talk to a passer-by: "Can't you just leave us alone to meet the people?" he asks a group of newsmen with some irritation. His protests are ignored, the pattern continues as before, through three or four shopping centres and a school. At the school, which the cavalcade has some trouble in finding because McCarthy doesn't tell them exactly where it is, he shakes hands with a few people, endures being mobbed by a crowd of curious children, and then almost without warning dives for his car and is driven off into the night. It has been a typical McCarthy campaigning evening.

Why does he do it? He obviously hates it. He looks embarrassed and hesitant every time he accosts someone. When he makes a speech at some little town hall, it doesn't matter that the crowd are keyed up to a high pitch of excitement and want to be inspired, roused, boosted: he will make a literate, clever but unexciting speech (punctuated by one or two dry jokes) which he will deliver as if he were reading the accounts to an annual general meeting. With his student workers, he will be quietly friendly, modestly encouraging, never over-excited—and they love him for it. But in the sort of phrase *Time* magazine

used at almost weekly intervals throughout 1968 : what makes
Êugene run?

I remember hearing him make a speech at a small college
in his home state of Minnesota in the autumn of 1967.
McCarthy, popular and highly thought of in his own area, was
already known for his opposition to the Vietnam war. The night
he came to speak, the hall was packed not only with students
but with scores of outsiders, even journalists from Washington,
who had come to take a look at the man who said "Boo" to
Lyndon Johnson. When he entered, he received a standing
ovation. His audience were keyed up for stirring words.

During the next hour or more, the tension and expectation
seemed to evaporate as if it had never been there. During the
course of McCarthy's speech, and during the questioning afterwards, it became clear that he was by no means in favour of
an unconditional withdrawal from Vietnam. Indeed, the burden
of his remarks seemed to be that the President was not working
hard enough to get negotiations for peace started, that the war
could not be won militarily—but that it was quite impossible
to withdraw unconditionally from South East Asia. When he
had finished, the applause was polite but subdued. When he
departed—to announce a few days later that he would be entering several primaries the next spring—he left many of his young
admirers feeling very frustrated.

For McCarthy then as now seemed to suffer from the failing
that makes many academics unconvincing statesmen : he was
too good at seeing both sides of an issue, of reducing black and
white to the grey that it probably is. That autumn, the vast
army of the young and many others disenchanted with the war
were looking desperately for a leader on whom they could
focus their beliefs. Senator William Fulbright, until then the
most famous Vietnam "dove", always seemed to prefer to do
his dissenting within the Senate Foreign Relations Committee,
of which he is chairman. Furthermore, as Senator for Arkansas,
although his personal views are known to be liberal, he has
been publicly illiberal on the matter of race relations—for
reasons of political expediency. Other notable opponents of the
war like Benjamin Spock and General James Gavin, the former
distinguished paratroop commander, lacked credibility as
political figures.

Then, when McCarthy announced that he considered the

President's war policies distinctly ill-advised, the anti-war party fell upon him as the Messiah. A Senator of long service and some distinction in a quiet way—most of his good works not being of the kind to catch headlines—he had the one quality the anti-war group had hitherto lacked : respectability, total and convincing. You might disagree with McCarthy, you might think he was splitting the country unnecessarily and dangerously, you might think he was politically naive. But it was very hard to argue that he was either stupid or irresponsible. From the day McCarthy started making noises in opposition to the war, he was gradually pushed by his supporters to an attitude which sounded a good way to the left of his original pronouncements, but nevertheless the one which was to hurt Lyndon Johnson so badly in New Hampshire.

I think annoyance may have played a considerable role in Eugene McCarthy's behaviour during 1968 : annoyance at the insults which were hurled at him when he announced his original reservations about the war; annoyance when Robert Kennedy entered the Presidential race so soon after McCarthy had paved the way in New Hampshire (for Kennedy had previously disappointed all McCarthy's public expectations of support, while promising that he had no intention of opposing Lyndon Johnson); and annoyance at Kennedy's very condescending behaviour towards him during the primary campaigns. McCarthy is a man of considerable personal pride and strong personal conviction. Since Senators command a very powerful political position in America, it seemed unlikely that McCarthy's existing career could in any way be damaged even if he were completely crushed in his primary jousts against the Administration. And it was clear at a very early stage in the game that anti-war feeling was sufficiently strong for McCarthy to be able to conduct some kind of campaign, whatever its outcome.

When the Senator announced his intention to challenge the President, it indeed looked like a contest between David and Goliath : but one with the important qualification that David could not lose. He could be crushed in his attempt to succeed, yes—but it was difficult to see how he could have ended up worse off than he started, except for some possible slight loss of face, which could be quickly forgotten in admiration for his courage.

Then, with McCarthy's outstanding performance in New

Hampshire, the gamble ceased to be a gamble, if it ever was. For whatever happened to him thereafter, he had made his point. More than that, his campaign had acquired an impetus and a credibility (that phrase was never far from people's lips in 1968) that ensured that McCarthy could not be taken lightly again. He had established himself, if not as a serious Presidential candidate, at least as a very serious factor in the Presidential campaign.

His young followers' ranks swelled with every day; his finances, while never all that bright, were greatly improved. It was true that Eugene McCarthy had gone in as a one-issue candidate (indeed two of his aides quit later because they considered he did not emphasise the racial problem sufficiently in his campaign). But it also became clear that many people voted for him in New Hampshire not so much because they agreed with his stand against the Vietnam war, but because they wanted to express some kind of demand for change. Change that is, of personalities, approach, attitudes—perhaps more than anything on the theory that no one could be handling the nation's problems as badly as the Johnson Administration seemed to be. Throughout the early days of the McCarthy campaign, long before enough was popularly known about his personality to make personal judgements really possible, the Senator was assisted by the simple virtue of being a new face. I don't think the importance if this should be under-estimated, since the polls consistently indicated that while very many people thought the Vietnam war was being mishandled, relatively few indicated a desire to see America withdraw unconditionally. I think that the importance of McCarthy as a new kind of politician, with his quiet and more or less subtle witticisms instead of the crudely humorous name-calling, was probably at least as successful as his political views in gaining him his popularity.

By March 31st, the day that Lyndon Johnson announced his withdrawal, there was every sign that McCarthy would win a numerical as well as a moral victory over the President on April 2nd, the day of the Wisconsin primary. The Administration, in the fortnight before, had unashamedly put a great deal of effort into winning over the Wisconsin electorate; and yet still the opinion pollsters told them that they were likely to lose. Once again, the question was asked: what difference does it make since the President still seemed assured of re-nomination? But

Johnson's opponents were greedily anticipating the new humiliation for the White House.

The morning after the President's withdrawal broadcast, which had caught McCarthy amazed, as he was addressing a meeting in Wisconsin, I was flying from Washington to New York to Senator Robert F. Kennedy, at that moment closer to the Presidency of the United States, it seemed, than ever before in his political career. It was as close as he was ever to be. It was April Fool's Day.

At 10 a.m. in the Overseas Press Club, there was total chaos. Kennedy's press conference had been scheduled before the last night's news broke, in a room that would comfortably take the thirty or forty pressmen who could be expected to attend a routine briefing. Now, with the Kennedy campaign hardly a fortnight old, it had suddenly assumed the shape it would maintain until the day of his death, with more than two hundred top-line reporters from all over the country squashed like sardines into every corner and dribbling out into the hall as Bobby entered. Fighting and swearing in a way that looked rough even for the New York press, cameramen struggled to be within shooting distance of the possible next President of the United States.

Kennedy fought his way in, had to pause before reading his statement while his audience stopped fighting and shouting. It was a shambles. Kennedy's key aide, Theodore Sorensen, who never looks a ray of sunshine, was standing behind his candidate looking as if he were attending the day of judgement. When the statement was read, it said nothing : only that Kennedy intended to request a meeting with the President (he got it, but nothing very useful seemed to emerge), and that he admired the courage of Johnson's decision. The questions afterwards were parried, and no one was very satisfied. After half an hour Kennedy and his wife Ethel departed, to disappear for a few more hours before he was due to hit the campaign trail again. He didn't look like a man whose chief obstacle in life had just been swept away. Rather, he resembled a bad case of shell shock.

But then one considered Kennedy's self-chosen election role : he had offered himself as the man of conscience who felt obliged to put forward an alternative to a President whose policies were opposed by a significant proportion of the electorate. Now, suddenly, instead of being the weaker man coming late to the field to fight all the political power than accrues to an incumbent Chief Executive, he was tilting at windmills. It was as if the Trojans had opened their gates after five years of siege and told the Greeks they'd had enough. Kennedy, sitting in his apartment in United Nations Plaza, must have been very unsure whether he was facing colossal good fortune or disastrous anticlimax.

That afternoon, while his chartered campaign plane was making the short hop south to the suburbs of Philadelphia, we were looking at Robert Kennedy very differently from the way we had done a few hours before. Yesterday, he seemed just an interesting outsider, whose presence in the Presidential race heightened the tensions and changed the odds a little. Today, he had become the possible next leader of the Western world. He didn't look very convincing material.

Outside supermarkets, in halls, in a stadium, he made a series of speeches that in a calmer moment would not inspire a woodlouse. But this wasn't a calm moment. He reeled off his standard lines: "We can do better", "I need your help", and the teeny-boppers mobbed him. They tried to clamber aboard the car as it stopped under floodlights in the street, shake his hand, grab a shoe, touch him and scream louder than their friends about how much they love Bobby. His grin looked toothier than ever. Standing on the platform while he was being introduced by another speaker, one couldn't help thinking that he looked like an industrious schoolboy taking a bow at prize-giving.

But the image, the charisma, were enough. The crowd scenes filled the screen on next day's TV newscasts, with the cheering and shouting on the sound-track almost obscuring his rather insipid remarks. Flying back to New York that night, he seemed to have cheered up somewhat from the morning. He was not a man who appeared to like people as individuals, but he did appreciate a good crowd. Now he was smiling a bit more, talking a bit more, even managing to sound interested when a few of the reporters on the plane chatted to him on the concourse at La Guardia airport. He had settled down somewhat. There must be many more meetings, many more decisions, many more cheering crowds. But the prize, that night, must have seemed tantalisingly attainable. And if he could not win now, it must have seemed highly questionable that he ever would.

. . . This was Kennedy on April 1st, 1968. Unlike McCarthy, Kennedy had gambled a great deal: to be beaten in 1968 seemed disastrous to any prospect in 1972. He no longer faced Johnson head on, but it was already clear that Hubert Humphrey would gather up much of the support that would have accrued to the President. He faced the handicap of divided forces: so many of the young who would almost automatically have joined his forces were deeply committed to McCarthy. It's said that many of his advisers opposed his entering the race at all. As he began to prepare his forces for the primaries in Indiana and Nebraska, where for the first time he would meet McCarthy head on, the omens may have looked better than they did on March 31st—but not that much better.

Kennedy campaigning mesmerised the nation. Partly because of the echoes of his brother that haunt Americans whether they liked him or not, and partly because Kennedy on the move is an amazing spectacle: the fantastic energy with which he travelled and fought for days on end, apparently almost without sleep; the crowds who tore off his shoes, cuff links, tie—anything they could seize—in his motorcades; the image alone of a Kennedy in the midst of the fray. He had the tremendous advantage of being able to draw vast audiences who, whether they supported him politically or not, were unable to avoid a chance to see a legend in the flesh. *Time* magazine reported during his Indiana campaign:

"Kennedy has invested prodigious sums of money in planning and publicity. He has also drawn upon that other great family resource: Kennedys. Pitching into his campaign, which included a whistle-stopping run across the state last week aboard his special "Wabash Cannonball Express" were wife Ethel, brother Teddy, sons David and Michael, daughter Courtney, sisters Pat Lawford, Jean Smith and Eunice Shriver, sister-in-law Joan, mother Rose and dog Freckles."

Who could resist such a spectacle?*

* For those who doubt the entertainment value of an American election, I quote from the almost endless list of show business celebrities who were giving their services to one or other candidate, performing in concerts to raise money, campaigning etc.

But listening to Kennedy making his speeches across the nation, I don't think it was just political naivety that made one wince at the speed with which he would change tack. In the ghettoes and in the East, the emphasis was on getting out of Vietnam and dealing with urban problems. In more conservative Indiana and Nebraska, it was "lawlessness and violence will not be tolerated", and promises of a much greater role for free enterprise and less for government in solving city crises. He appeared almost to ignore McCarthy, his rival in the race, while pressing hard his key point of the need for a change, for a new America with new leadership. Since both Nixon and Humphrey undoubtedly looked somewhat shop-soiled after their years of appearance and re-appearances on the political scene, Kennedy again enjoyed the same advantage as McCarthy: he might not be a new face, but he looked a young, fresh one.

Kennedy won in Indiana and Nebraska, by reasonable if not decisive margins, because he was far better known and far better organised than McCarthy. He was able to buy more television exposure—and there's no possible doubt of the tremendous importance of television in America elections—and his campaign was in the hands of a top-class machine. In Indiana, it was said with some satisfaction, the lazier local newspapers were printing word for word hand-outs prepared for them by the industrious Kennedy men. McCarthy's personal organisation was in dire trouble, especially since its main professional prop, Richard Goodwin, had defected back to the Kennedy camp after the Wisconsin primary. And Kennedy always possessed the subtle

For Kennedy	For McCarthy
Warren Beatty	Theodore Bikel
Henry Fonda	James Coburn
Gregory Peck	Eartha Kitt
The Supremes	Peter, Paul and Mary
Sonny and Cher	Paul Newman
Andy Williams	Jose Ferrer
Sammy Davis	Walter Matthau
Jack Lemmon	Myrna Loy
Sidney Poitier	Tiny Tim
Barbra Streisand	Eli Wallach
Rod Steiger	James Baldwin
Tony Curtis, etc., etc.	Mary McCarthy, etc., etc.

In 1968, Hollywood, not to mention the literary community, closed ranks behind one candidate or another at an early stage in the game.

but highly significant advantage of being a convincing Presidential candidate: one could easily imagine another Kennedy in the White House. But McCarthy? Somehow, it just didn't seem right.

McCarthy's holding actions in Nebraska and Indiana (and undoubtedly Kennedy hoped to beat him so shatteringly in one or both of these as to smash him out of the race), leading up to his amazing victory over Kennedy in Oregon at the beginning of June, were a triumph of energy and personality over heavy odds. His own quiet style continued to appeal to voters who found the Kennedy circus an extravagance (remember that it was perfectly possible to write-in a vote for Hubert Humphrey if one liked neither Kennedy nor McCarthy), and his young campaigners behaved with an enthusiasm, courtesy and a charm that almost compensated for the poor central direction.

This was the keynote among the students working for both Kennedy and McCarthy: once inside the political framework, they played the game by its rules. At a McCarthy headquarters in, say, Omaha, Nebraska, one might find everyone sleeping on the floor, dressed like hippies, bearded, long haired and superficially anarchist. But they were working for something—something very specific and tangible, something many of them had hitchhiked or ridden by bus for hundreds of miles to participate in. They performed with an intelligence and enthusiasm, not to mention obedience, which impressed the voters on whom they were working as much as it baffled their own parents.

It was, if anything, much less complicated to believe in McCarthy than to believe in Kennedy. McCarthy was a college professor of modest origins, quiet courage and conviction, fighting heavy odds for what he believed in. With him there existed an unspoken rapport, a link that was all the more valid because they shared it with him alone. But Kennedy could never entirely escape all the old stigmas of ruthlessness and exploitation. It was very hard to forget his old associations with the arch anti-Communist, Joseph McCarthy, nor the saying: "He's more his father's son than his brother's brother". McCarthy suffered in elections because he lacked Kennedy's idolising following in the ghettoes (in Oregon, where he won, there is little ghetto life), but Kennedy's broader base of support meant that he had less time and immediate contact with his student following. Still, it was amazing to see the extent to which Kennedy could exist on the unseen magic alone. I remember one notable occasion, again in Omaha, when he addressed a small Catholic college in the city and made one of the finest speeches of his campaigns. Standing there in his shirtsleeves, he did not flatter or cajole them. He asked them why they were not out doing something to make America a better place to live in. He browbeat them, in many ways he puzzled them, but he showed a force and a feeling which all too often seemed lacking in his public appearances.

No one could doubt how much Kennedy cared about the injustice and misery in America. His problem was that so often he behaved as if he and only he knew that it existed and was capable of changing it. It's said that he was genuinely puzzled at the anger his entry into the race in the wake of McCarthy's trail-blazing provoked. All too often he seemed to see the world through his eyes alone and forget that others had eyes too. Yet in the latter half of his primary campaigns he became noticeably more attractive, because he did try to face some of the old Kennedy stigma and laugh at himself a little.

"I'd sent my brother Teddy to New York to collect some campaign buttons for me," he was saying one day, "and when he came back, I found that he'd had his face put on all of them. I told him it was no good, of course. It was too late for him to enter the race. And anyway—people'd say he was ruthless. . . ." Everybody laughed, everybody liked Kennedy so much more when he was able to make remarks like that.

Because I only spoke to him myself two or three times, I was neither assisted nor hampered in writing about him by any knowledge beyond watching him in action and talking to those who worked with him and covered him. Because I liked McCarthy so much as a man, I had been as critical as anyone in discussing Kennedy on the campaign trail. But one night in Nebraska, when the results of the poll were coming in, I was standing by the stage in the press room as Kennedy waited to be interviewed on television. Sitting there on the steps, while a make-up girl tried to take the shine off his face, he looked more than tired, he looked . . . old. Yes, a little old, rather worried— all the clichés that have ever been used about him : tortured, driven, uncertain. I don't know whether watching him there made one more sympathetic or less so. The press corps who travelled with him on all his trips liked him very much indeed.

Indeed, Murray Kempton seemed to put it so well when he said later that, in the business of writing about Kennedy as a Presidential candidate, he felt deeply sad that he'd never taken the chance to tell him how much he liked him. It seems pointless to dwell at length on Kennedy's character, because this has been done so often by many others much better qualified. But I found it impossible to escape the fact that even when well accustomed to dealing with politicians and politics, in the presence of Robert Kennedy, one was very conscious that one was in the presence of a legend—whether a good or bad one doesn't matter.

Eugene McCarthy once wrote : "American liberalism can be a positive force for good only if it clarifies its positive content and becomes something more than the liberalism of the immediate past. Optimism, generosity, tolerance and even humility, good and necessary as they are, are of little use unless there can be some agreement as to what is good."*

What distinguished the battles of Kennedy and McCarthy in 1968 was that in their different ways they seemed to the young, and to more than just the young, to be getting close to some agreement as to what was "good".

A writer in the *New York Times* looked at McCarthy's peace campaign early in the spring : "At its best it has been something special, something very rare in American politics. It has been a grass roots movement that defied the pollsters and the pundits to spark a political revolution. It has been a crusade—and that is the only word, for there has been a religious fervour in the air —that united thousands of people, not by the charisma of an Eisenhower or a Kennedy, but by a common belief in what Eugene McCarthy calls 'the best of all causes, the cause of peace'."

In a strange way—and I advance this notion hesitantly—it may have been better for us all that Eugene did not become President. For such is the nature of political necessity and reality, it is not as easy as one might like to think to change the course of the country at a stroke. How much would change if McCarthy became President (or had Kennedy) will remain a mystery. It's doubtful how much original thinking McCarthy has to offer on the problems of the cities or domestic unrest, far less whether he and the Negro communities could ever have

* *Frontiers in American Democracy* by Eugene J. McCarthy, published by World Publishing Co., New York, 1960.

achieved anything approaching real understanding. But as the leaders of a great new political movement within America, albeit an unsuccessful one in gaining the Presidency in 1968, they generated a faith which has not been sullied by the practical tests of power. How much will linger on to 1972 and beyond remains uncertain.

On the morning of June 5th, 1968, when I picked up my telephone and heard of the tragedy in Los Angeles, I remembered Kennedy being asked by a nun at some campaign meeting whether it was true that he favoured donating blood to the Vietcong. He put his hand to his face and choked: "Oh my God! And you're wearing a Kennedy button?"

I remembered Kennedy being asked what he had that McCarthy hadn't—except money—and replying with that brash grin: "Charm, sense of humour, and of course I think McCarthy is basically ruthless".

I remembered asking him a question and hearing him say: "It's too early to say . . ." Now, it was too late ever to say . . .

These were all the trifles, so insignificant and so transitory. Watching a funeral at Arlington Cemetery, seeing the President once more saying the same things in the same atmosphere as only two months before, trying to avoid crying not only for Kennedy but for America, it was not until much later that one realised that a second phase of America's election drama had already ended with the California primary—even in the hours before the assassin punctuated it with an unthinkable full stop.

In the previous pages of this book, I've been considering almost exclusively the events and personalities which made headlines in America 1968. This seems a good time to turn aside from the centre-pieces of the year for a moment, and look at America as most of it is: far removed from the centres of news and politics, only aware of disaster thanks to television and the papers. I travelled in thirty-six of the fifty states at one time and another, and met all kinds of Americans. I remember a rice farmer in Arkansas who was driving myself and some colleagues somewhere, and who suddenly paused to point out a local landmark: "That's a liquor store!" We looked suitably impressed, but obviously somewhat baffled. He explained further. "It's privately owned—no government control or anything . . . you don't have them where you come from, do you?" He was under the impression, it transpired, that he was escorting three hard-line Communists. Nor was he alone in his misapprehensions.

In a nation where Congress pays a great deal of attention to the views of its constituents in considering social legislation— and the House of Representatives is weighted heavily in favour of rural areas—the people's view of the domestic situation can carry great weight. Opinion polls have revealed that at one time recently seventy-five per cent of the population felt that the Negro was being brought forward too fast. This percentage has rarely dropped below half, and members of Congress remember it when civil rights legislation is brought before them.

The phrase, "the average American", makes commentators shudder whenever they hear it used; if there is any country where there is a truly "average man" it is not the United States, with its regionalism and immense breadth of opinion and varying ways of life. In trying to assess how Americans feel about their country and its role and its problems, I can only cite personal experience in conversation with hundreds of people all over the country. The picture may not be a fair one, but it is the nearest I can achieve in viewing America as she entered the latter half of a traumatic election year.

CHAPTER 6

THE BACKGROUND: WASPS STILL STING

"You can't understand how strong a grip this war has on
us, you know. Why, Vietnam is like . . . like a pet charity!"
Minnesotan lady at a Minneapolis dinner party

JUST WHAT, PRECISELY, is the "American Dream"? Everyone has his own definition. But perhaps the best interpretation
would be to say that it is a vision of an America that is God's
country, a land blessed by fertility and beauty in incredible
abundance, into which have been thrust vast numbers of people
of very diverse backgrounds, to make of it what they will.

Make of it what they will. . . . Perhaps that's the key: perhaps the strongest motivation for so many Americans is the
belief, borne out by the evidence, that if they have the brains
and the guts and the will they can achieve anything they want
to, regardless of their origins. And correspondingly, if one does
not succeed, there is the belief, regardless of the evidence, that
it is because one lacks the will, the drive and the guts. That it
is, in other words, one's own fault.

How many times in America does one hear a successful
businessman say: "If *I* could do it, why can't *they*?" He ignores
the fact that he was born in an age where education was far less
important than it is today, that in an age of specialists he is
asking why a man who did not complete high school is unable
to build a fortune. He is more than likely to add that "all this
business about racial prejudice gets exaggerated. I'd hire a man
to do a job regardless of his colour, if he had the ability." When
he says that, he is being patently unreasonable, since discrimination in jobs and in housing is still rife. Surveys show that
Negroes in Chicago, for example, may be better qualified than
white men but are getting lower pay. Nevertheless, the businessman believes that the opportunity is still there to be taken if a
man has the initiative. It would be easy to say that this stems
from deliberate blind selfishness, which perhaps it often does.

But there is also a faith which goes a good deal deeper. It is a faith which not only accepts but cherishes the ideal of independence, of self-sufficiency, and is very upset when this is threatened. In particular, when it's threatened by government control and higher taxation (Americans complain constantly about their "high" taxation, which is in fact so much lighter than our own). Talking of the "dispossessed", the old middle class who feel their status threatened by the changes in American society, the sociologist, Daniel Bell, wrote :

"The common denominator of such groups is the life-style and value of Protestant Fundamentalism—the nativist nationalism, the good-and-evil moralism through which they see the world. Theirs are the values of the dominant thought of the nineteenth century; and they have been defending these values —in what is now a rearguard action—for the last forty years."

If, as Bell suggests, their struggle is indeed a rearguard action, to a visitor to America it seems a very convincing one. I've never forgotten my first weekend in America, at a party in Connecticut, being slapped on the back by a vice-president of a major American company, and told that "Our two great countries should join together to prevent the Russians from taking over the world". A colleague of mine was dining one evening with an extraordinarily pleasant Mid-Western couple, when the conversation turned to race. "What's to be done? We can't shoot them, we can't send them back to Africa, we can't sterilise them—it'd be against the law. . . ." The husband was asking the question not in anger, just with a sense of sad frustration.

Perhaps it was hearing many, many remarks like that which prompted a civil rights leader to say that he was sick and tired of investigations into what was wrong with black society, and wasn't it about time someone got down to investigating what's wrong with white society? This may also be part of an explanation as to why so often Negro Americans are much better company than whites: they have a cynicism and freshness of approach which, constructive or otherwise, at least makes conversation a lively exchange.

For while it may be true that it is poor whites, jealous of their status in both the North and South of the United States, who put much of the venom into race relations, it is also true that the more affluent and better educated whites seem unable or unwilling to lead them the other way. The WASP—the

White Anglo-Saxon Protestant American—has traditionally looked downwards on minorities, whether immigrants from Eastern Europe or Negroes, and one of the most ludicrous features of city life in many parts of America is the WASP country club. Many, in their frenzied search for some kind of social exclusivity to support their inherited or self-made wealth, still exclude Jews as well as Negroes from their membership.

Listing the apparent aims of middle-class America, especially rural middle-class America, one might place :

(1) The preservation of personal independence, e.g. low taxation and minimal interference in local affairs from the Federal government.

(2) The maintenance of law and order, the suppression of riots, etc.

(3) The continuation of the fight against Communism, providing this does not require too great increases in taxation or loss of American lives.

The second point, which deserves more attention a little later, is closely bound up with the first. In an extraordinary exercise of logic, many Americans seem more than willing to spend large sums on expanding the police forces, sending in the National Guard to quell disorder, and on law enforcement in general, without being willing to consider the causes of crime and riots. Statistics which show that the vast majority of all crime is committed by the most under-privileged section of the population make no impression when suggestions are made that improving their lot might help deal with crime. Each riot has caused a great dilemma as to which is worse : living in fear of more trouble because ghetto conditions are not improved, or living in anger because the rioters have been "rewarded" for their misdeeds by getting better conditions. I touched on this problem more fully in Chapter 2.

American social commentators will remind you that while the nation may not yet have a welfare state, immense progress has been made in the last thirty years, and the country has already been moved from dogmatic attitudes which seemed almost unshakeable. But perhaps because the gulf between America's promises and the realities has never been wider, it is impossible to avoid feeling that the country is still reluctant to face the reality that the aristocracy of talent with all its vast rewards has failed as badly as ever did an aristocracy of birth. More so, indeed, since an aristocracy of birth at least contributed some stability to society, for better or worse. But the social and physical mobility of America's aristocrats of talent—come to that, the mobility of everyone in the nation—makes the stability that stems from a sense of "belonging" somewhere almost impossible to attain. Many arguments have been advanced to show causes which contribute to America's present restlessness, most of them valid. Historically, Americans have always had the feeling of having room to expand, room to move around in, room to move in every sense, physical and mental. There's no doubt that today there is an increasingly uneasy feeling that the country has run out of room to expand, strange though this at first sounds, when one considers the vast tracts of virgin land in so many parts of the country. Possibly the unease stems more from the feeling there is nowhere to go which is uncontrolled, unhampered, unregimented—until very recently there have been many such places within the continent. Perhaps, and one doesn't say this in any way unkindly, Americans have started to get an uneasy feeling that they are "like everyone else"—and for a country to which nothing had hitherto seemed impossible, this must be a sad revelation.

The chaos of the Vietnam war, which has gradually slipped into every American's consciousness in a very special way—the frustrating evidence that the greatest power on earth cannot accomplish its military wishes; the turmoil in the cities which is still only half glimpsed in so many American homes; the disaffection of the young, for whom to know more than their parents is to see the world more critically than their parents : all of these things have had their profoundly disturbing effects on the ordered pattern of middle-class life, in the suburbs that is, of course, since in America so few people can live in the country, and so few wish to live in the squalor of the core cities.

But perhaps a part of the tragedy of the riots in the cities is that they seem to have stifled any existing conscience about the lot of the Negro, despite the part they played in drawing public attention to the critical nature of the situation. The riots have enabled WASPs, and white Americans at large to find a measure of self-righteousness which has been reflected in 1968 in the campaign platform of Richard Nixon, and which has further encouraged Congress in its parsimonious attitude to funds for the war on poverty. Immediately after the President's anouncement of the setting up of a Commission to Consider Violence in the United States, the following reader's letter appeared in the columns of the *Washington Post*:

"So we are to have another Commission! This can only be a Commission to investigate, then confirm the previous Commission on Crime. This current multi-million-dollar decision is broadcast to the nation with the same parrot-like speech we heard so many times before.

"Then we hear tear-jerking comments of TV newsmen who try to outdo each other in an effort to dramatise the sickness of all Americans. As they so emotionally indicate, every man and woman of America must take credit for the sickness and crime we have today.

"As an American-born citizen, I consider this a grave insult. I do not approve—nor support—an Administration whose only answer is to pour more millions into the pockets of Commission members and compiles reports—reports which require ages to unravel, and which are interpreted by the Liberal Establishment for the public. We can expect to await breathlessly a year or two for the determinations the Liberal Establishment make, the most impressive of which will be the appointment of Commission members to judgeships, or some other top post.

"I am one citizen of approximately half this great nation who voted against the type of Administration we have today. From those I talk with from day to day, I am not alone in resenting the blame placed on every American for the crime that has grown immeasurably under our present so-called leaders. I especially resent being blamed for a crime (Robert Kennedy's assassination) that is a direct outgrowth of the Establishment's liberalism and laxity. It is none of my doing, none whatsoever!"

I quote this letter at such length because it reflects so accurately many of the comments I have heard made, more or less forcefully, during 1968. A point of view with which I suspect the above writer would agree was expressed more calmly by Barry Goldwater in his book *The Conscience of a Conservative*:

"Liberals... in the name of a concern for 'human beings', regard the satisfaction of economic wants as the dominant mission of society. They are, moreover, in a hurry. So that their characteristic approach is to harness the society's political and economic forces into a collective effort to compel 'progress'. In this approach, I believe they fight against nature."

Goldwater, who, one might mention as an aside, is a man of remarkable charm and courtesy, uses the phrase "in a hurry" in such a way as to imply that haste is in itself a vice. His conviction in this direction is taken even further by such right-wing groups as the John Birch Society and the Minutemen, who assume that all change must be change for the worse. Such groups have assumed a new, if idiosyncratic, prominence in the past few years.

And while not many Americans would care to go all the way with Barry Goldwater, less still with the extreme right-wing fringes, very many indeed believe that the Government in Washington is in far too much of a hurry to change their society. The most notable shape this belief has assumed is dislike or even outright hatred for the United States Supreme Court. If the Congress is always one step behind the people's thinking, the Supreme Court has in the 1960s been consistently two steps ahead. Such decisions as that which ruled it unconstitutional to make schoolchildren attend the customary morning prayer meetings, and which narrowed police powers to interrogate suspects, have aroused very many Americans to a high pitch of indignation. A bill in the Congress which would have effectively overturned several recent Supreme Court decisions was only narrowly defeated, and President Johnson's hasty nomination of liberal Abe Fortas as the new Chief Justice, before this power passed into other and possibly conservative hands, provoked much unfavourable comment. Many Americans consider the Supreme Court has been dangerously overstepping its powers: the South has traditionally loathed the Court and all its works since the early desegregation decisions from that body, and now the North too, in a new flush of conservatism, is expressing its displeasure. How far the present mood will go it is hard to say. But one long-time observer of the Washington scene, to whom I was expressing mild surprise at the ultra-liberal character of some new Court decisions, remarked thoughtfully: "Right now, I think the Supreme Court is holding the line against some very nasty forces indeed". It was the possibility of these forces gaining further ground that induced Johnson to try to secure the Court before his own departure—Justices holding their posts for life, Earl Warren offered his retirement to make way for a younger man.

But while much of the nation hankers for tougher courts to deal with rising crime, and a Supreme Court which appears less eager to appease the law-breaker, there is no sign that Americans are prepared to take their police more seriously, or do anything to encourage them except to provide them with more men and more lethal hardware. Most Americans I met regarded the police with mixed fear, dislike and contempt. The police return this feeling in due part by an apparent complete lack of self-respect and an indifference which turns occasionally to active unpleasantness towards those they are supposed to serve. When I first arrived in America and happened to mention Vance Packard's study of American social life *The Status Seekers*, I was quickly given a lecture on its inaccuracy and misconceptions. But while Packard may have his shortcomings as a sociologist, nothing I saw in the months that followed contradicted any of his findings as to the materialism of status in the United States. It is, after all, only in very recent years that academics have come to be regarded with any kind of respect by most Americans. And today it is still true that the policeman, so low in the economic scale, is treated with all the contempt due to one who has taken the job—it's assumed—because he is incapable of doing anything that pays better.

My own encounters with the American police were on the whole friendly until Chicago (see Chapter 9). And in one very affluent suburb in which I stayed, I remember asking whether a party guest would lose his licence driving home in his rather shaky condition, but was assured that the local police would simply chauffeur him home if they stopped him. There is no question about the fact that pillars of society are treated with the respect their influence can command. But equally, the relationship between the police and the population in less affluent areas —notably, of course, the ghettoes—is almost universally bitter. Ignorance, prejudice and simple brutality have done as much as anything to create the climate for the urban riots: indeed, many of those that have taken place were sparked off by incidents between police and ghetto residents.

In 1968, the arms race in the cities assumed new and more formidable proportions, as police forces all over the country armed themselves for trouble: armoured cars, anti-sniper teams,

assault rifles, tear gas, Mace disabling spray, body armour—
these are the answers to the problems in the cities. A police chief
like Frank Rizzo in Philadelphia takes great pride in the formidable and ruthless anti-riot force he has assembled. "If we have
a riot in Philadelphia," he says wolfishly, "it'll be the shortest
in history."

The suburban population approve. The fear of a riot in
which the mob leaves its own areas to attack white neighbour-
hoods had led a Detroit motor executive I met there to buy a
gun after the disorders of 1967, although he admitted he had no
idea how to use it. "I owe it to my wife and children," he said.
In Memphis, the day of the March in memory of Martin Luther
King, a taxi driver who was bringing me in from the airport
said: "You won't catch me working when the March is on. I
live in an area all surrounded with nigra homes. I'm going to
lock myself in with my rifles" (he said he had three) "and goddam anyone who tries to come near me. I got my children to
think about. . . ."

Nor is it only fear of riots that induces Americans to arm
themselves. The volume of crime involving firearms has led
many businessmen and householders to buy weapons. It is estimated that there are anything up to two hundred million guns
in America—one for every head of population, man, woman
and child. When Robert F. Kennedy made a speech pleading
for gun control in Oregon a fortnight before his assassination, a
man shouted from the crowd: "Hitler's rule in Nazi Germany
started with the registration of firearms!" The main lobbying
group which is very effective in preventing serious firearms
control legislation is the National Rifle Association. Suggestions
to their members to write to members of Congress when some
new control legislation is proposed almost invariably produce
massive and successful results. The NRA is strongest of all in the
rural areas, in states where shooting is popular. It's hopeless to
suggest that it is possible to have gun control without banning
sporting shooting: gun control of any kind is anathema in the
eyes of hunters and, to city Americans, would merely deprive
the lawful of self defence while leaving all the massive supplies
of guns at present in circulation at the disposal of criminals.

I remember one occasion when I'd stopped at a petrol station
late at night to ask the way, and after doing so, pulled round
the pumps to wait for a friend who had retired to the washroom

at the back. When he eventually returned, we were about to drive off when he drew my attention to the petrol pump attendant. The latter was standing half in and half out of the door, covering us with a revolver. He continued to do so until we drove off. He seemed to think that we had plans to hold him up.

On another day, I was being driven through New York state by a senior magazine executive, who was telling me about his collection of one hundred and fifty guns. One hundred and forty-eight of them he kept at home, he said. The other two? In the interests of "self-protection", he was carrying one loaded .38 revolver in the pocket of his Cadillac, and another on his hip.

In Houston, Texas, which with a total of 244 murders in 1967 was the murder capital of America—the figure is higher than that for the whole of England for the same period—I heard a television newscaster end a bulletin with a joke about the manner in which someone had been shot the night before. The appalling aspect of the situation is the number of unpremeditated murders which would almost certainly not take place were a weapon not readily available. A marital quarrel can have a very speedy end indeed, if both parties know that there is a loaded revolver—"for burglars"—in the top drawer of the bureau.

If there is one respect in which it's clear that America *is* suffering from a very serious national malaise, it is in the matter of firearms. The number of deaths each year which occur as a result of spontaneous fire from a police officer—"in the line of duty"—is bad enough. But it's obvious that matters have gone much too far now to disarm the American police. What can and must be done is to disarm private citizenry, and destroy once and for all the masculine mystique regarding firearms that America clings to as a hangover from the days of the Old West. The existence of this mystique is *not* a myth : as a casual visitor, one saw too much of it to think that. It's a menace. The number of accidents, never mind murders, that take place in the shooting field of America each year, is catastrophic. Once again, this is at present taken for granted. The right of one American to shoot another without let or hindrance seems as firmly guaranteed by the Constitution as that of free speech. If the Founding Fathers had anticipated the outcome of that fateful phrase in the Constitution : "The Right to Bear Arms". . . . You really can buy an anti-tank rifle that is advertised as "ideal for long range shots at deer", you know.

Watching the day-to-day life of an American suburban community, however, the only likely intrusion of such matters as firearms is when one hears that Mrs. X is recently widowed since her husband drowned while out duck shooting. (I met such a widow.) Even forgetting the areas I visited where there was a lot of loose change even by American standards, the first thing that must strike any outsider is the affluence of so many of the homes. While household help is almost unobtainable in many places regardless of what salary is offered (domestic service is so low on the status scale that it is the last resort for most working people), the amount of gadgetry and machinery, comfort and gloss to be found in many middle-class homes overwhelms a foreigner. Once again, so much has been written with such accuracy about life in American suburbia that it doesn't seem worth repeating. It's enough to say that one is surprised, first, by the speed and amount of alcohol consumed on a day-to-day basis and second, by the total cultural void which seems to exist once one leaves New York until one reaches San Francisco and the West Coast.

More important are the attitudes of reasonably prosperous businessmen who will play such a large part in running their city or area. In the rural areas where there is only a small percentage of Negroes, and no ghetto, the most oft-repeated conviction is that the cities are no concern of anyone but their own inhabitants. Most of all, country towns resent angrily the idea of any Federal tax increase which might be called for to finance city development. It is in the small towns most of all, not unexpectedly, that the idea of the American Dream remains strongest, and the war in Vietnam is most determinedly upheld as part of the vital battle against "the Reds". In the course of dinner in a small town in South Dakota or Texas, I've heard theories suggested about America's role in the world propounded that would make the old British Empire sound a modest proposition. The higher the casualty figures from Vietnam, the more the military handling of the war is criticised. But the price being paid makes the people all the more determined to see the nation emerge with some tangible reward for the blood that has been spilt. Very many Americans believe that their country should have deployed its full military might in Vietnam long ago, invading North Vietnam if necessary, taking whatever risks seem desirable in provoking the rest of the Communist bloc. Always, always, the question is asked of a European : "Why do you all hate us so much when we try so hard to protect your interests?" Always, the reminder is made that America came to save Europe in World War II, with the implied rider that we've never been properly grateful. These people are puzzled, unhappy, aware somehow that something is wrong, but utterly determined that their nation and the sense of values they think it represents should be preserved—by whatever means are available. Their communities tend to be over-age, because so many Americans are leaving the land—farm prices are very low and agriculture seems to offer little profitable future when there is so much surplus production—and the young are migrating to the cities for the higher paid jobs in industry and business. And yet, even allowing for all this, there are very many small towns all over Europe which have a charm which is wholly lacking in American rural communities. Perhaps it's just that because of their newness and yet oldness, they have all the vulgarities of American big cities, with no corresponding compensations.

Turning to the big cities and their suburbs, one finds among the more important businessmen a growing awareness that they have a responsibility to the ghettoes and their inhabitants. In more and more of the bigger cities, business men are making efforts to recruit Negroes as never in the past, to train them for jobs and to pay them a reasonable wage. But as mentioned earlier, unless these efforts are on a far greater scale than at present envisaged, it's hard to see how they can help solve the urban crisis anything like fast enough. Perhaps, however, it's hopeful enough that some kind of will is at last emerging—for this was lacking for so long.

Lower down the economic scale of the white community, it is obvious that the will is still lacking. Open Housing has been one of the key issues in the civil rights struggle during recent years—the demand that a man selling a house should not be permitted to discriminate in deciding to whom he sells it. The latter part of 1967 saw one civil rights leader, Father James Groppi (referred to in Southern newspapers as "The mad priest of Milwaukee") leading a long series of major demonstrations in that city, pleading for open housing. Milwaukee has a size-able population of Eastern European immigrants of fairly recent extraction, who cling desperately to such status as they have finally achieved by escaping from their ghettoes, which were abandoned to the incoming Negroes. This section of the population led the anti-Open Housing element, and although they are now technically defeated—the Open Housing law was passed in Congress after Martin Luther King's death and a series of long delays—the situation remains unsettled. A union official in another Mid-Western city told me that three families had recently moved out of his modest suburban street after a Negro family moved in. Such determination is still very common, and acts of violence to deter Negroes moving into white neighbour-hoods are quite commonplace. The Negroes I met living in white areas appeared to have succeeded in finding a modus vivendi mainly by being neither seen nor heard. The opportunities for evading the Open Housing law when it comes fully into force seem almost limitless, and this appears likely to be a troubled front for as long as there are white men who feel a social stigma in living next door to a Negro.

It's one of the strangest aspects of the racial situation in America that although Negroes account for only about eleven per cent of the nation's total poulation, so many whites remain convinced that the Negro is in some way a threat to their society. This very real fear of a serious Negro revolt on a large scale seems all the more absurd when one considers that the white establishment hold "every card in the deck".

"Put it this way," said one Negro journalist who was taking me round Harlem, "even if the Negro community rebelled and sat down to withstand siege within their own areas, they could hardly keep going for long on the contents of the local super-markets. On practical grounds alone, it's hardly possible to start a rebellion in a city."

This, of course, ignores the much simpler fact that the Negro communities in American cities lack the will and the ability to do much more than burn some buildings, commit limited acts of wanton violence and frighten the daylights out of a white community who are all too willing to be frightened.

There really does appear to be substantial evidence that once Americans are convinced a danger exists, their opinion is very hard to shake: once Senator Joseph McCarthy had persuaded the nation that it was threatened by Communists in the early '50s, it was a long time before he could be discredited. And even now, the feeling that the Vietcong's attacks on Saigon somehow endanger Los Angeles is implied in much of the discussion about Vietnam between an outsider and an ordinary American. This same ill-articulated but powerful fear of the Negro characterises many of the white dealings with the ghettoes. Young Negroes exploit this when they see a stray white man in their area. They will test his reactions—daring him to be afraid. Laugh at them, clench a fist and yell, "Black Power, Baby!" and they'll laugh back (that's not to say that one isn't frightened anyway). But the white attitude of greeting the Negro as a strange and probably dangerous creature from another planet has done as much to create the present racial situation as treating him as an inferior human being.

The problem of a society in which affluence, social structure, and inclination have placed the white middle class at the safest possible distance from the kind of tragedies and crises which faced America in 1968 was brilliantly expressed by Malcolm Muggeridge in a recent article:

"Everything is known about everyone; nothing is hidden. Yet I had the same feeling this time" (visiting America) ". . . that somehow what is seen and heard and reported belongs to an elaborate fantasy, with little or no connection with what is really happening.

"There is so much power and so little strength, so much wealth and so little ease, so much information and so little knowledge. A great and widening abyss, as it seems to me, yawns between the happening and the recounting; between the event and the image, the achievement and the dream. In the vast and intricate process of news, the news gets lost; within seconds of the bullet entering Martin Luther King there is no bullet, no King, only a story."

The fact that millions of Americans spent so many hours this year mesmerised by minute-by-minute television coverage of national events makes strangely little difference to the degree of ignorance so many of them reveal about the simplest facts of, say, ghetto life or the problems of poverty. Many Americans continue to refuse to believe that any of their countrymen are actually starving. It all seems such a long way from Peyton Place.

"It is not that Americans have changed so very much," wrote Margaret Mead, the sociologist, looking back over the last twenty years. "What has changed is the world itself and our ability to comprehend and act on our comprehension of this changed world."*

Amidst so much in America 1968 that almost made one despair of finding the will for change in many sectors of society, it was tremendously comforting to find a number of prominent men determined that much must be changed. Perhaps the most outstanding was—and is—John Lindsay, the Mayor of New York. Lindsay has been accused of being an impractical dreamer, lacking the practical ability to make things work : but especially in the past eighteen months, in times of riots and fear, Lindsay has proved himself a man of extraordinary personal force. He has established a rapport with the ghetto inhabitants that would have been regarded as impossible if he had not proved that it could be done. He has produced some long-term ideas for the future of great cities that are much criticised largely because they show how much must be done. He has brought the energy and enthusiasm into urban planning that seems sadly lacking elsewhere in the United States.

"The best motto for a Mayor of New York," he says, "is 'Shoot your wad and get the hell out of it'. It's a job you should approach every day, not caring how many enemies you make, and it's a job you should be prepared to regard as a dead end."

Hardly; many Lindsay supporters are already eyeing his chances as a possible Republican Presidential candidate in 1972, and it was said that he might have been Vice-Presidential candidate in 1968 if he had really wanted the job. The key to Lindsay's theme song about the American cities is that they need very large sums of money from the Federal government—who have been slow and reluctant to realise that city taxation is grossly inadequate for city needs—and that they must have a much greater degree of self-rule. At present, he is hamstrung financially because he must seek money from the Legislature of New York State, who refuse to antagonise voters by taxing the largely suburban population to aid New York City. In the drive to bring new life into his city centre, Lindsay has been offering every possible incentive to manufacturers to come in and set up shop, and has even been trying to relax city rules

* *And Keep your Powder Dry* published by Apollo Press, 1965.

about film-making to encourage Hollywood to come to New York for location shooting. He says of Congress :

"I don't think these people have the feel of city problems at all. They haven't got the soil, or rather the concrete, in their boots."

He is experimenting with new prefabricated housing units that can be lowered into the shells of sub-standard buildings (obviously, a potential short-term aid to improving the housing situation). He has managed to weather a corruption scandal involving one of his top officials which many people suggested would break him—they seemed to enjoy it all the more because of his overt determination to kill City Hall corruption. And he has apparently avoided becoming disastrously involved in any factional warfare within the Republican Party—although his liberalism is inacceptable to the most ardent of the party faithful. Most of all, he has single-handed done an enormous amount to keep New York "cool". He walks the ghetto streets alone when there's trouble, because to go in with a police escort would be to incur certain mistrust. One day during the summer, when a policeman accidentally killed a Negro youth (having missed another youth the shot was intended for), it was Lindsay who went in to talk to the mob that gathered, and got a cheer by the time he left. Lindsay is every political engineer's dream : strikingly handsome, an ex-naval officer and lawyer who skis, swims, sails and plays tennis—indeed, that angular face and the blue-grey eyes have probably won him more support than his policies. But Lindsay, to an outsider, seems to have the compassion and the understanding of a Bobby Kennedy with, more important, the apparent practical ability to implement his ideas without appearing a professional hatchet man.

These remarks, to a skilled observer of New York politics, might seem over-ecstatic when one considers the problems Lindsay faces, and the obstacles in his path. But I admire Lindsay because he appears so totally uncommitted to the old American ideals which cripple so many of that nation's politicians. He is willing to try anything if it works. He is not glancing over his shoulder with constant nostalgia to the days when a man could "move West" when things began to get complicated.

But perhaps even more important than those who were finding a new perspective on domestic issues in 1968, listening to men like Lindsay and looking to ways other than brute force to bring peace to the ghettoes, were those who saw America's international role in a new light. The academic community were, in general, opposed to the Vietnam war and all it stood for long before Eugene McCarthy and the Vietcong's Tet offensive made others think further than the top of their flag-pole. But while there may be no great surge of demand for unconditional withdrawal from Vietnam, if ever that tortuous misery can be ended, it seems that the casualty figures have done what all the lectures and persuasion could not—convince a significant number of Americans that a route other than force of arms must be found by which to deal with the Communists. They may not like the Communists any better, they may be unwilling to be defeated by them once committed, but there may in the future be less talk of the virtues of pre-emptive war against China, of the desirability of keeping the Russians at bayonet point.

The great question-mark which overhangs all this, however, is whether the end of the war could also herald the beginning of a new phase of isolationism. Very many Americans feel deeply hurt at what they consider the "ingratitude" of the rest of the West to their struggle. They are even more wounded by the abuse hurled at them by countries which receive massive American aid. The cuts in foreign aid in 1968 may have been partly inspired by the national economy drive, but there is no doubt that the decision was publicly popular for moral as well as financial reasons. Few serious American politicians believe that America could ever isolate herself again in the manner of the post-World War I era (although some have been urging the creation of new protective trade barriers). But Americans, hitherto anxious to help at every opportunity, whether mis-guidedly or not, feel that they are getting scant thanks for pulling the capitalist world's chestnuts out of the fire. Small-town Americans are likely to make this very clear to their repre-sentatives in Washington for some time to come.

How did all this affect the American voter in 1968? It gave rise to a story quoted in *Time* magazine, of the opinion pollster in the Mid-West who asked a voter in the street whether he would vote for Nixon or Humphrey on November 5th, and got punched for his trouble. Puzzled, the pollster asked him, why the fuss, he was going to have to vote for one or the other?

"Yes," replied the voter. "I know. But I don't like to be reminded of it."

It would be difficult—impossible, in fact—to say what the American electorate wanted to be able to choose from in 1968. They hardly knew themselves. But it was abundantly clear that in times which frightened and disturbed so many of them with such good reason, they wanted to be offered a face and a man who seemed able to lead them clear. Nixon and Humphrey, old men of American politics both, seemed to offer traditional remedies to maladies which had never struck so forcibly before. Some might like Nixon because he claimed to offer stability and firmness. Others might like Humphrey because he was an old-line Liberal, battered by time, but a man who fitted a well-established mould. It was just that well-established moulds were not enough. Whatever people's personal convictions, there was a profound sense of disappointment in the air as it became clear that neither Rockefeller nor McCarthy could break their rivals' stranglehold on the national party conventions. They felt that, somewhere, a chance had been lost.

This situation is very difficult to articulate, because it is not easy to see the compatibility between those who disagreed with many of the attitudes of Rockefeller and McCarthy, and yet only knew for sure that they did *not* want Humphrey or Nixon. It came back once again to Theodore White and his remark about great issues contested by disappointing candidates. Nixon and Humphrey seemed the essence of mediocrity. The latter, especially, was the epitomy of the compromise candidate. As June and July moved on, spasmodic violence might flare and die away in the cities, politicians might race around the hustings crying their wares. But the curious sense of vacuum increased.

Remembering the America that braced itself for autumn in 1968, there were momentary thoughts and recollections that emphasised the character of both the year and the society that faced it.

A brief newspaper item from the spring:

"A businessman who shot and killed his mother-in-law and critically wounded her doctor before shooting himself, was described as an avid gun collector upset by the move for more rigid firearms laws . . . a neighbour said he had been disturbed since the slaying of Martin Luther King. 'He has a valuable gun collection,' said the neighbour, 'and he was disturbed over the clamour for rigid gun control legislation. He felt that the registration and other requirements were unnecessary'."

Arthur Miller, the playwright, writing in the *New York Times* after Robert Kennedy's assassination :

"Because America has been bigger on promises than any other country, she must be bigger by far on deliveries . . . between the promise and its denial—there stands the man with the gun. Between the promise and its denial stands a man holding them apart—the American. Either he recognised what he is doing, or he will take the final, fatal step to suppress the violence he has called up. Only justice will overcome the nightmare. The American dream is ours to evoke."

Of personal memories, one remembers examples of the anomalies of the United States: a day in Arkansas when I attended Governor Winthrop Rockefeller's annual cattle sale at his country estate, an occasion which brings together two or three thousand of his constituents for a great free jamboree. Watching Rockefeller jovially addressing them all after lunch, one was aware of a sense of semi-feudalism about the atmosphere which I've never seen in England.

And yet such is the division of power in the United States that almost the entire nation must be convinced of the rightness of a decision affecting domestic life before it can be executed.

So many Americans are baffled by the interest we take in their doings, seem unaware that they hold the power of light and darkness over us all. And yet so many, on hearing one comes from England, will show keen interest in recalling that their great-great-grandfather came from Leeds. Thinking of that, I remember that when I met George Wallace he spent five minutes telling me about the Anglo-Saxon and Celtic backgrounds of himself and his wife.

Then there were those who would argue passionately the case for encouraging the Negro to return to Africa; and yet again those who turned out one spring day in the New York ghettoes to help "clean the place up". The trouble was, although they were so gay and so willing that day, not many came again.

. . . Anomalies and half-truths, dilemmas and half-decisions— where does one begin to see which is the real America and the

America that will be in the future? Once again, it's a personal question which must be answered from the evidence, confused, fragmented, unsatisfying though that may be. Perhaps that is the way to remember America in late summer, 1968 : confused, fragmented, and unsatisfied. One must also add, from a personal viewpoint, deeply depressing.

For the vast majority of Americans, the poverty of some of their fellow-countrymen is not something they see every day, it is a story they read in a newspaper or see in an occasional television documentary. The war in Vietnam they must interpret from the nightly TV newsfilm and the pictures in Life magazine. In 1968, the news media in America assumed an even greater importance than ever before in shaping opinion, giving the nation vital information hour by hour, and presenting the personalities and events of the Presidential Election. A Roper Research Survey found that while in 1959, Americans receiving news of a major event regarded newspapers as more credible than television by a margin of thirty-two per cent to twenty-nine per cent (radio and magazines making up the difference to one hundred per cent, in 1967, television was the more widely accepted by forty-one per cent to twenty-four per cent. In the under-35 age group alone, a Nielsen Audience Survey in 1967 found that male Americans watch 3.11 hours of television a day, women 4.18.

These figures alone suggest something of the impact of the media, some of the reasons why it would be hard to discuss American opinion and thought in 1968 without considering the means by which they receive their information.

"I suppose you're here to do one of those 'Oh, my God, the Americans' stories," a magazine photographer remarked bitterly to me in Memphis after the assassination of King. Should the American media be doing the "Oh, my God, the Americans" stories? And are they?

CHAPTER 7

A MESSAGE FROM OUR SPONSORS

"Any appraisal of political candidates or their remarks by television newsmen would constitute a cardinal sin against the medium's most holy commandment: *Thou shalt not offend.*"

Gene Wycoff in *The Image Candidates,*
Macmillan, 1968

"THERE IS SO much information and so little knowledge . . ." suggested Malcolm Muggeridge. Being involved in the business of newsgathering, it is part of one's job to attempt to absorb as much as possible of the information available in newspapers, magazines, and on television and radio about a subject in which one is interested. In America, the quantities of material of every description are intimidating. First, any observer interested in what is going on around the country must attempt to read the *New York Times,* the *Washington Post* and the *Wall Street Journal* with the greatest possible frequency. He must study the weekly news magazines, *Time* and *Newsweek.* He may look at the photo-magazines and the glossies, *Life, Look* and the others. He should see *Congressional Quarterly,* a weekly survey of the political situation and the background to legislation being discussed in the White House and in Congress. Every evening, he should watch the half-hour television news reports of one or other of the major television networks. If there are any special documentaries being screened, they probably justify a glance. There are the political periodicals like *New Republic,* and the reports constantly appearing from private and government organisations on poverty, race, the Vietnam war. There is the endless stream of books on current events appearing within weeks of their taking place. There are the special supplements on the nation's problems which appear in Sunday newspapers, adding even greater poundage to editions which already require a real effort to carry about, they are so heavy. How on earth, in the face of this constant barrage of news and information, could anyone *not* have a reasonably balanced view of what is going on around him?

Part of the answer must, of course, be that as in any country at any time, the vast majority of the population are not interested in working through more than a tiny fraction of what is available. The character of American society, however, accentuates trends even though they also occur elsewhere : the total predominance of the television habit ensures that for most Americans this is the major source of opinion-forming news. Beyond television, they may read their local newspaper with a greater or lesser degree of interest. They may subscribe to *Time* or *Newsweek*. But it is much more likely that having read the social column in the paper, they will move on only to the *Reader's Digest* or *McCall's* women's magazine.

The size of America makes the existence of true national newspapers like *The Times* or the *Daily Express* in England impracticable. The great American newspapers, like the *New York Times* and the *Wall Street Journal*, the *Chicago Tribune* or the *Washington Post*, enjoy a degree of national distribution which usually makes it possible to buy one or more of them a day late on the other side of the country. But most Americans derive their daily written news from one of the hundreds of local newspapers across the country, which vary enormously both in size and quality. The only national newslinks are the material provided by the national news agencies, notably Associated Press and United Press International, and the articles by the top columnists like Art Buchwald and Joseph Kraft, which are widely syndicated among both large and small newspapers.

All this apart, however, one must always return to the major source of information : television. Across the United States, there are some 644 commercial television stations, varying in size from those covering the huge cities with audiences in millions to those in small country towns reaching only a few thousand viewers. Although the air waves are now getting increasingly crowded, anyone with the money to start a station who can find an area which does not appear fully covered can apply to the Federal Communications Commission for a licence. The system of control over station owners must surely be the loosest in the world. The requirements for serious programme content are often only marginally observed. The numbers of advertisements per programme is far higher than in England, and is indeed causing some experts to believe that the public is getting annoyed at their frequency. The profits for those with a stake in television and a little business sense are fantastic. American television is, from a business and ethical standpoint, wide open.

The broadcasting pattern is geared to the three great national networks, NBC, CBS, and ABC. These three, in addition to owning some stations of their own, syndicate much of their material across the nation to stations affiliated with one or other of them, though financially independent. These affiliated stations (450 out of 644 are affiliated to one network or the other) carry material from the national networks for about sixty-five per cent of their total air time. During the remaining hours they broadcast, they carry an average of seventeen per cent of films, 13.3 per cent of local material, and 4.7 per cent of assorted videotape shows they have purchased.

To explain something of the financing of American television, let me offer an approximate and fictitious example of how revenue is gathered and divided up. A big motor company pays, say, NBC $175,000 for the right to sponsor an hour-long television show which will be carried by all NBC's affiliated stations at a peak hour. The motor company will also pay out perhaps $200,000 to finance the production of the show. The revenue paid to NBC will be shared with affiliated stations; NBC might give a reasonable-sized city television station $1200 for carrying the show. In addition, the local station can insert some of its own local advertisements in between the motor company advertisements in the programme, and keep the entire revenue from these for itself.

This example is slightly abnormal only because sponsorship of whole shows is now so expensive that many companies only sponsor part of a given programme. But the financing, correspondingly divided, remains the same.

To offer a different kind of example, however, I can quote some accurate figures on the hard cash of one not untypical small-town television station in the Mid-West. Its owner purchased it for one million dollars. It costs him 750,000 dollars a year to run. Its revenue each year is around a million. Not a bad return on an investment, since although taxes must be paid, television is an area where it is notoriously easy to juggle accounts.

One further side of American television I have failed to mention—the Education Network. Many big cities now have educational TV stations financed variously by public and private money. In New York, there is also a Public Broadcasting Laboratory, established with a ten million dollar grant from the Ford Foundation, whose programmes are carried by many educational stations around the country. PBL was set up to try to prove that given adequate money and without the millstone of advertising, television could be good. And indeed some fascinating programmes have emerged. Much of what is good in American TV appears on the educational networks, it is just that most local educational stations are so poorly financed and equipped that it is impossible for them to experiment greatly. And the audience figures remain pathetically small.

Thus television is dominated by the great networks. Vast sums of money are involved in their operations through advertising. And most important of all, advertisers have great influence on what appears. It is often argued that English commercial television panders to the lowest common denominator of its audience. I can only say that is is far, far better than American television in this respect. While here, the success or failure of a programme in the audience ratings may determine its success or failure, this is far less directly related to the whims and wishes of advertisers.

In America, a show very popular in the ratings last year was *The Smothers Brothers Comedy Hour,* basically a variety show into which the stars had slid some satirical overtones—satire, however, very mild indeed by British standards. By the end of the show's 1967–68 run CBS, who were networking it, were experiencing some difficulty in keeping advertisers interested, despite high ratings. CBS censors attended every run-through and insisted on deletions of a kind which would be laughed at in England. Specifically, a storm arose about the Smothers Brothers' desire to have a folk-singer named Pete Seeger on the programme. He is an excellent performer, but since the 1950s has been blacklisted by all American TV networks for having alleged Communist affiliations. When eventually he was permitted to appear, CBS insisted that he did not sing a protest song about the Vietnam war—"Waist Deep in the Big Muddy,

And the Big Fool Says to Push On". By this time, the row was public knowledge, and gained such publicity that Seeger was eventually invited to appear again and sing his song. But it was impossible to know whether to laugh or cry about the genuine air of crisis and worry which had developed around the question of whether CBS dared to let him sing or not.

It would be unjustifiable to suggest that the networks permit advertisers to interfere directly with the contents of news programmes. But it is indisputable that the difficulty of getting sponsors greatly reduces the number of serious documentaries being made for showing at reasonable peak hours. Sometimes, the networks make and air these at their own expense, as a concession to morality and current affairs. But more often, they will merely appear at infrequent intervals during afternoon or very late night viewing hours. The discussion programme of a serious nature is effectively non-existent. There are endless "talk shows" but these usually entail either show business interviews, or political figures being asked questions by a TV personality obviously illiterate in current affairs. Writing in his book *The Image Candidates* about television's handling of political candidates, Gene Wycoff says:

"A station that offered information, no matter how valid, that sharply contradicted a political candidate would run the risk of offending that candidate's supporters. That station might become 'controversial' and scare away the advertising agencies, whose dollars are the lifeblood of television."

It takes very little to make a television station or national network "run scared". At the national level, how much safer it seems to screen *Bonanza* and *Gunlaw* round the clock than risk a hard-hitting film on poverty! Indeed, when one network did screen a documentary of the latter kind, government officials descended in full fury, accusing them of inaccuracy and overstatement and misrepresentation. It was questionable who was more surprised—the viewing public to be told in between Westerns that poverty existed in America, or the parties involved that a network had had the courage to be controversial.

The Vietnam war is said to be the first war in history that has been brought home to every American—literally—by the television news film which appears nightly on the screen. This is indeed so, and it is undoubtedly true that the sight of such films has done as much as anything to make many Americans critical of the Administration's handling of the war (and pathetically anxious to compromise—trying to achieve success without incurring the casualties inevitable if the gloves are taken off).

But whether television has truly represented every aspect of the war, and viewed the entire situation in a reasonably critical light, is another matter altogether. The army's reports of massive Vietcong casualties are broadcast without comment or scepticism. It is rarely that the handouts on "successful offensive drives" are offered to the viewer with any really searching analysis of the facts presented. Walter Cronkite, the most successful television news-presenter, went to Vietnam himself to report, and sent back some films and opinions which cast doubts on American policy. It was not the fact that he did this that is cause for surprise—it is the fact that America was enormously surprised that he had stepped so far into the area of controversy. Technically, the general standard of NBC and CBS's nightly half-hour news shows is excellent: good reporters, good films, highly professional presentation. But they never seem to go nearly far enough. Eric Sevareid is a professional pundit who each night delivers some thoughts on the news during the Walter Cronkite bulletin. Sevareid is clearly both articulate and able, but it is often embarrassing to see the lengths to which he will go to put both sides of an issue—and the issue itself is usually carefully chosen as one unlikely to offend any large section of the nation. Perhaps, the remark of Sevareid's I remember best came after the assassination of Robert Kennedy: "There seems little hope at this time of a successful mass self-psychoanalysis on a national scale". As with so many of the really good American television personalities, one can't help feeling that behind the network image there is somewhere a tough journalist trying to get out.

Far beyond the day-to-day operations of the networks, and of their restrictions, there is the routine censorship exercised by the local television stations. In the South, as I have mentioned, stations will almost invariably transmit an old film at any time the national networks are offering a documentary which might be thought to reflect on the honour of the Confederacy. In that part of the world also, there is positive hatred for Cronkite and Huntley-Brinkley, the news broadcasts from the East Coast, which Southerners consider are constantly providing unfair and unreasonable coverage of, say George Wallace or the treatment of Negroes by Southern police. There seems something so unjust about cameras being present whenever there is a confrontation between civil rights workers and the white establishment.

But censorship or, perhaps more kindly, selectivity, is exercised by stations all over the country in respect of films or news shows. A Milwaukee station not many years ago refused to carry the Melina Mercouri film *Never On Sunday,* on the grounds that it was immoral. And as the Smothers Brothers' found out, never try to do a skit on smoking and cancer when there's a chance a cigarette manufacturer might be available as a sponsor.

At the local level, also, one particularly unpleasant form of journalistic corruption is that of permitting local newscasters to advertise products in between reading items. It seems questionable how much faith a viewer can place in the integrity of a reporter who, in between giving him "the facts", will hold up a packet of detergent and extol its virtues. This practice is still widespread, although not among the national network newsreaders.

In the end, television in America must remain a totally lost cause as a useful means of creating knowledge and understanding unless there is some drastic reform of the structure. There is, at present, virtually no personal scrutiny of any applicant for a licence to broadcast, to discover whether he is in any way a responsible person to control a local station. The regulations setting out the minimum serious programme content are grotesquely inadequate. And only an infringement of the financial or technical regulations can get a station licence withdrawn —rarely if ever is such action taken because of deplorable programme content.

There must also, surely, be some way in which advertisers can be torn from their present stranglehold on the entire medium. As long as controversy on a network is enough to make an advertising agency run to cancel its contracts, there can be no chance of offering Americans a reasonably stark look at problems and alternatives. At present, television's main contribution to the American domestic scene has been on the one hand, as the arch-propagandist of the American Dream in all its dangerous obsolescence and, on the other hand, as a significant agent in showing the nation's underprivileged what they are missing in the way of Scandinavian furniture and holidays in Hawaii.

During the year's great tragedies, television's coverage of assassination and disaster, funerals and processions, was technically superb. Vast resources skilfully deployed made millions of Americans live these experiences as never since the death of John F. Kennedy. The story told itself—the incredible dignity of the thousands of Negro mourners at Martin Luther King's funeral in Atlanta, the horror of the scene in Los Angeles, the night of Robert Kennedy's death—all this shook the nation deeply. But is this enough? It's very hard to believe that it is.

Thus, if most Americans want strong guidance in their political and social thinking, they cannot look to television for it. But no such delicacy of approach affects local newspapers. I look at these first, because while upper-echelon executives, academics, and professional people may read the *New York Times* or the *Wall Street Journal,* the local newspapers play the greatest part in bringing written news to those lower in the economic scale. In general, it is depressing to find just how illiberal most small-town newspapers are—in other words, how accurately they reflect the natural feelings of their readers. Even when they are not doing this, when their audience is less hide-bound, many of the proprietors still try hard to turn the clock back. Perhaps most famous of all is William Loeb, owner of the New Hampshire paper—the *Manchester Union,* who at Primary time every four years attracts considerable attention by invariably urging his readers to vote for whichever candidate is aiming furthest right, and by doing so in strongly worded terms.

The correspondence columns of local newspapers are always, in a rather chilling way, good value : letter-writers are likely to be urging everything from sending Negroes back to Africa to dropping the atom bomb on Hanoi. Foreign news is almost completely excluded, although there may be a series running daily with a title like "Our Boys Over There" with profiles of local men fighting in Vietnam. The sentiments expressed in leader articles may be little different from those of readers writing in the correspondence section. Indeed, the only breath of outside air probably comes from the syndicated national columnists : a man like Art Buchwald writes too amusingly to be excluded merely because he is a liberal.

It is all the more unfortunate that the big city newspapers do not reach far into the country, because papers like the *New York Times,* the *Washington Post* and the *Wall Street Journal* (somewhat specialised though the latter is) are so good (the *Los Angeles Times* is not quite so high up in this category). The *New York Times* and the *Washington Post,* especially the former, carry an enormous amount of information, have excellent foreign news services and brilliant leader writers. The *New York Times* leaders, notably liberal, are frequently making headlines elsewhere in the country because of the influence of their pronouncements. All American newspapers seem to suffer somewhat from the "group journalism" concept, which gives little opportunity or incentive for individualistic writing from the humbler staff reporters. But the top writers are more than good enough to compensate for this, especially in the coverage of the political campaigns on a day-by-day basis. The *Washington Post*'s continuing battle for effective gun control legislation, and the *New York Times*'s constant critical reviews of Vietnam policy put them many lengths ahead of most American newspapers. American papers often suffer badly because they carry little material from foreign sources—offer little in the way of "outside looking in"—but the *New York Times* printed Harrison Salisbury's dispatches from Hanoi. It is not relevant in this context to attempt an assessment of the relative merits of American newspapers—sufficient only to say that in an ocean of mediocrity, the aforementioned three take all the honours. There are a handful of others—smaller, even more regional papers—which also make a notable contribution to sane commentary and coverage. But one is left with an overwhelming impression of a large number of American newspapers which still pay overwhelming homage to Mother, the Flag and apple pie.

Two interesting developments in the American newspaper world, however, took place in 1968. One was wholly negative: a lengthy shut-down of all newspapers in Detroit, Michigan, because of a strike. It took only a few days of the months the strike lasted to prove that no news, given the existing climate of fear and apprehension in American cities, is worse than bad news. Despite an increase in television news broadcasts in Detroit and the establishment of a "rumour office" which citizens could ring for accurate information on rumours they had heard by word of mouth, the city became a hotbed of suspicion and worry. The white population, already thoroughly alarmed after the 1967 riots, were very ready to believe any alarming reports on the situation in the ghetto, and the Negroes, conversely, were quick to accept any stories of whites perpetrating outrages on blacks. It is frightening to speculate on the possible course of events had a riot occurred in the city during the strike : television men would have had their work cut out to convince the city that the Russians had not landed.

Another newspaper strike, in San Francisco this time, was responsible for a more positive achievement. The local educational TV channel, already well known as one of the best in the country, started a "newspaper of the air", using many of editorial personnel from the newspapers made idle in the strike. The project was an overwhelming success, and audience ratings for the channel rose sharply. Although the strike is now over, further development work on programmes of this kind is continuing. Anything which serves to lift television coverage from its groove must be regarded as very hopeful.

The other highly significant source of news for most Americans is the weekly news magazine. *Time,* much bigger in circulation than *Newsweek,* is also much more highly opinionated. It has made its huge success largely by a publicly-declared policy of not attempting to publish news but "news as we see it". *Time* is immensely readable once one has adjusted to its slickly racy style, and editorial self-satisfaction. But while *Time* specialises in major analyses of the state of the nation, backed up by massive research and an apparently reasonably liberal outlook, at the end of a rather solemn article on the need for re-evaluation of traditional values, one is left curiously unmoved. There is a strange feeling that it's all addressed to someone else. I don't mean that because I'm an Englishman—after a year in America, one can hardly feel totally detached from the country's situation—indeed it's a comment I've heard Americans make as well. Underlying *Time*'s superficial air of critical examination is a comforting feeling that it's all going to be all right in the end. Perhaps when a publication is as successful as *Time,* it's hard to feel otherwise.

Newsweek, on the other hand, while it bears a strong superficial resemblance to *Time,* tries much harder to separate editorial comment from factual reporting. *Time,* covering the elections, has a genius for digging up the most amusing stories, the smartest cracks. But to discover precisely what was going on, it was often more satisfying to turn to *Newsweek*. The news weeklies—and for this it is hard to blame them—seem to forget much faster than anyone about the events of the week before. How easy it is to forget riots and assassinations when, only one issue later, there is a fast-paced and witty *Time* story on what the Presidential candidates are doing now! Yes, life must go on even after a tragedy, or a series of them.

But is it wholly desirable to return as fast as possible to an attempt at complete normalcy? It was the same on television during the rough days of 1968: the screen would be filled with the story, largely uninterrupted by commercials, for two or three days. Then, acutely conscious of the agonising amount of revenue lost in that time, the companies were back with their old films and the advertisements for deodorants. Once again, was I being oversensitive to wince when the television schedules were restored to normal so few hours after the horrors of Robert Kennedy's assassination? Indeed I remember, while we were waiting in acute suspense after the news came that Martin Luther King had been shot in Memphis, there was more domestic comedy and a fistful of commercials before the awful bulletin announcing he had died.

In the later days of 1968, all the American media became noticeably sobered by all that had happened, so much of which many of their staff had been covering at first hand. The Riot Report had concluded that there were far too few Negroes in the media, and that coverage of the ghettoes was at best half-hearted. All the best newspapers and television companies began a determined effort to improve on past performance. After the tragedies and assassinations, newspaper reporters excelled themselves—the best like Jimmy Breslin and Mary McGrory, writing brilliant dispatches from Los Angeles after Robert Kennedy's shooting.

But at the end of the day, looking not at the stars of American journalism or at the outstanding TV documentaries but at the general daily information presented to the American public, one is left with the conclusion that something, somewhere, is still very wrong. Broadcasting is a self-castrated eunuch. Most newspapers lack the spirit of national self-examination on which all the best must work. It can easily be argued that many of the criticisms I have made are as true of other countries, other media. But is this an adequate answer in a nation with the resources to do it better, and a crying need to improve the education of the people, not in terms of adding two and two, but of adding black and white, communism and capitalism?

Between the assassination of Robert Kennedy on June 5th and the opening of the Republican convention on August 5th, there was another of 1968's merciful lulls. The Democrats battled on among themselves: Eugene McCarthy's victory in the New York primary provoked more bitter party in-fighting, while Nelson Rockefeller's campaign for the Republican nomination flickered unhappily in the shadow of Richard Nixon's triumphal progress.

Hubert Humphrey's every syllable was pounced on by the political analysts in the hope of finding some nuance that might suggest a break with Lyndon Johnson's policies, but few such signs were to be detected. In New York, Mayor John Lindsay was called forth once again to break up yet another near-riot in the Harlem ghetto by sheer force of personality, while in Cleveland Black Nationalist Ahmed Evans led a group of his followers in a murderous attack on the police which left eleven dead on both sides. The Vietnam war dragged on, playing its unwelcome background symphony to America's domestic unease, and Congress sat in Washington almost motionless. One of the most powerful reasons advanced for making some changes in the nation's election system is that during a campaign year, almost the entire legislative and decision-making process grinds to a halt. While the politicians spend months on end discussing the problems and issues, nothing is being done at a practical level to solve them.

The two political conventions provided observers with contrasting kinds of misery: Miami was merely a ritualised spectacle being performed in the nastiest imaginable setting; Chicago, in four days, reminded one of all the reasons for finding America in 1968 a very frightening and unpleasant place.

CHAPTER 8

MIAMI TO CHICAGO

"We ought to quit pretending that Mayor Daley did
something that was wrong. He didn't condone a thing that
was wrong. He tried to protect lives."
Vice-President Hubert H. Humphrey
after the Democratic national convention,
September 1st, 1968

PEERING OUT THROUGH the morass of vulgarity that
is Miami Beach, Florida, an American journalist expressed his
astonishment that the Democrats, with their natural talent for
the obscene, had failed to choose the city for their convention.
Miami is the city where the Coca-Cola culture of the clichés
attains its nadir. It is the gathering point for all that is com-
mercialised, all that is second rate, all that is a living lie in
American society. As that same journalist went on to add, the
Republican national convention looked entirely at home there.

During the space of this book, little has been said about
either Republicans or about Richard M. Nixon as a contender
for the Presidency of the United States. To some extent, it is
true, this is a result of personal prejudices. But far more, it is
because until August, 1968, the Republicans remained in the
shadows while the Democrats fought their bitter battles, and
Richard Nixon slipped on to the stage at intervals only by
default—because there was little else happening at the time.

But as the delegates to the Republican convention gathered
in Miami Beach on August 4th, and as at last their doings swung
into focus, it was universally conceded that Richard Nixon had
run a brilliant race. A man noted for making blunders at the
wrong moment, he had forced his path through this election
year without putting a foot wrong. Perhaps this was largely
by default, in that the ineptitude of his opposition had gained
him as much as his own manoeuvring. But then one had to
remember that in the autumn of 1967 Governor George

Romney appeared the front-runner for the Republican Presidential nomination, and Nelson Rockefeller's prospects were still being discussed in respectful terms.

The New Hampshire primary had provided no Republican fireworks, because Romney's demise had been the result of a process of erosion rather than a sudden deathblow. But after Nelson Rockefeller's active candidacy was declared, he had spent at least as much money as Nixon on promoting his cause, albeit with little effect. Nixon had triumphed through the primaries in the face of dubious opposition, yes, but also because of brilliant organisation and careful planning. He had timed his campaign to come to a spectacular climax in Miami Beach, so that, even as Rockefeller was still working frantically to rally delegates, Nixon's arrival in the city appeared every inch that of the conquering hero come to claim his rightful spoils.

Conventions rotate not around the convention hall, but around the headquarters hotels. It is in these that the hurried policy meetings are held, the reporters scurry in search of their stories, and the drum majorettes and girl volunteers prance with their ribbons and hats proclaiming support for one candidate or another. For much of convention week, Nelson Rockefeller's base in the Americana Hotel remained the focus of attention, if only because it was only his massive drive to break Nixon's grip on the nomination that seemed to have the slightest chance of success.

It is a journalistic habit that when one has said all there is to be said about the probable, everyone turns his attention to the possible. And never was this more true than in Miami. On August 4th, Richard Nixon's hold on his delegates appeared invincible. As a result, until the hour of the vote on Wednesday, the press corps was kept busy plotting every move of Ronald Reagan and of Rockefeller on the million-to-one chance that they might achieve the impossible.

The convention atmosphere was not a very happy one for anyone except the delegates. The combination of the pretensions of Miami and the total lack of political excitement reduced observers to a state of miserably frustrated boredom. In the heat and the laziness, it took a conscious effort of will to take an interest, and that interest stemmed only from the fact that Nixon was more than likely to be the next President of the United States.

He is not a likeable man. To an outsider—and to many insiders, too—he seems the epitomy of the plastic politician, the man who at the beginning of a campaign will feed all the data on public opinion on issues into a computer, and proceed to shape his own platform strictly on its findings. I remember laughing with everybody else at the time of the New Hampshire primary, when a political scientist remarked: "You know, I wouldn't be surprised if Dick Nixon emerges as the peace candidate in this election". And yet here we now were seeing him as presenting almost exactly that face. A hawk in domestic issues, more or less a dove on foreign policy, his genius at the Republican convention was to emerge on a platform so nebulous that anyone could interpret it exactly as he wished. He laid stress on his determination to get out of Vietnam, without saying how, and while the party platform stressed that there should be no "camouflaged surrender" there. He emphasised law and order at home, while adding that he intended to ensure that every American had a self-respecting job. Most of all, in his acceptance speech on the Thursday night of the convention, he sentimentalised at length on the "American Dream". Whatever else one may believe about Nixon, there can be no doubt that he is deeply moved at the vision of himself, the poor small-town boy from nowhere, emerging as President of the United States.

It was to this idea that he has returned constantly in his speeches and public pronouncements, and it is this idea perhaps as much as anything that gives him his continuing faith in the basic justice of American society.

So disjointed are American political conventions that it seems pointless to carry an account of the Republicans' tribal gathering in 1968 through its every stage. First, there are the committee meetings to work out the platform and the procedural details, then for the first three days of the convention there is an almost totally meaningless series of speeches from, to and for the party faithful. Dozens of men and women from small-town USA must be given a chance to boost their prestige before their local constituencies by saying a few words at national TV prime time. The motions of democracy must be observed, despite the fact that conventions very rarely serve as a forum for real political debate. Their function is to unify political parties which are almost totally fragmented except in election years, to bring together personalities who may never otherwise see each other, to rally everyone to the cause for the election fight ahead. They should also serve to heal internal wounds incurred during the battle for the party's nomination during earlier months, and in this the 1968 Republican convention succeeded admirably. Fearful of any repeat of 1964, when those who opposed Barry Goldwater within the party continued to do so right up to the November election, with disastrous consequences, in Miami the Rockefeller and Reagan factions bent over backwards to show their support for Richard Nixon, once he had achieved his overwhelming majority on the convention floor.

The minor battle that erupted on Thursday, when certain factions attempted to overthrow Nixon's announced choice of Spiro Agnew for Vice-Presidential nominee, melted away almost as quickly as it had begun. Mayor John Lindsay of New York made the seconding speech for Agnew's nomination, even though for many liberal Republicans, he himself would have been a far more inspiring choice for the role.

But this was not a liberal Republicans' convention. Many words were spilt during the week on discussing the differences between the Goldwater convention and the Nixon one. Listening to the flow of rhetoric from the platform in Miami, it was hard to discern any noticeable shift of mood. When Goldwater himself appeared to speak, he received a colossal ovation. When Nixon was debating between conservatives and liberals as to his Vice-Presidential choice, it was to the conservatives that he bowed. Indeed, perhaps the most noteworthy event of the convention was the "bugging" of a secret Nixon address to a group of Southern delegates by a Miami newspaper. The transcript revealed that in return for their support, Nixon was willing to go a very long way indeed. One of the "king-makers" on the convention was Strom Thurmond, one of America's most notorious long-time racists from South Carolina with whom Nixon appeared to be in frequent communication.

Each day immediately before the convention opened and in its first three days, Nelson Rockefeller held a press conference at his headquarters to announce progress. It was an almost embarrassing ritual, since on each occasion the same statement was made—"We are gaining ground. This will be an open convention. No one has anything sewn up yet"—and each time reporters asked for evidence of Rockefeller progress which he was patently unable to supply. Ronald Reagan seemed to manage his operations with more face-saving skill. Having only announced his active candidacy at the eleventh hour, in Miami itself, he continued throughout to follow the line that he was only offering himself because he had been under such pressure from his supporters to do so. When so thoroughly beaten on the convention floor, he seemed to have lost little, and if anything only gained considerable additional publicity for use in California, by having projected himself on to the national scene. The mere fact that his activities had been so extensively reported and so seriously treated were a measure of the astonishing success of a man whose credibility as Governor of California had been often in doubt.

It dragged hideously and depressingly, that convention week. To a serious student of the academics of politics, conventions are a fascinating study. But approaching them at the most practical level of personalities and policies, there was little cause for celebration. The delegates appeared to be in a state of happy euphoria simply because they saw their party uniting once more, and with every prospect of victory in the November election. That same euphoria appeared to prevent any serious reflection on the nation's problems and dilemmas. 1968 seemed a time at which America was coming to Republicanism, rather than the Party needing to move itself towards the country. The basis of both Nixonism and 1968 Republicanism was the call for a restoration of peace and quiet at home, if possible, it seemed, achieved by a headlong rush back to the ideas and ideals of 1776.

Perhaps the best hope for Nelson Rockefeller and for the long-term interests of new thought was when the Democrats seemed to be ahead. There were three more or less clear phases to the year's politics: first, in the autumn of 1967 and early 1968, when the Republicans felt that any candidate they chose to put up could beat any Democrat—and certainly beat Lyndon Johnson. Under those circumstances, they would sooner have Nixon than anyone else as their nominee.

The second phase, which dawned with the spring, occurred when the polls suggested that several Democrats could beat Richard Nixon, while there was considerable evidence that Nelson Rockefeller could defeat them. At this stage, it seemed at least possible that the Republicans would choose Rockefeller, a likely winner, rather than Nixon, an apparently likely loser. But with high summer, Nixon's successful progress through the primaries, his improved standing in the polls, and the evident chaos among the Democrats all coincided to prove to the Republicans' satisfaction that it was indeed Nixon who was their "winner". Since this idea entirely fitted their own predispositions anyway, it was with a hearty sigh of relief and good cheer that they could welcome him into Miami Beach and give give him a warm send-off on his national election campaign. His choice of Spiro Agnew for a running mate seemed uninspired, but it was a measure of their confidence in Nixon's prospects that they felt they could allow themselves the luxury of rejecting a liberal.

This was the name of the game in Miami Beach : it was hardly a battle for power or, if so, one fought with pea-shooters; it was more a skilfully organised benefit match to kick off Richard Nixon's political season. The balloons were bursting, the bands playing, the delegates watching their strip-shows downtown, and such signs of discord as appeared were smoothed over as mere minor fits of pique. Nixon was being launched with a freedom of political manoeuvre that came from being given almost carte blanche by his party. He could say and do almost anything—and it would fit neatly into the airy pronouncements of the platform. All he had to do on his cross-country campaigning was maintain his energetic hammering at the need for change, playing the soothing tune of peace and quiet as his theme song to a nation that most of all wanted to be left alone. Nixon's message was kept as uncomplicated as possible, because the thing Americans have resented most deeply in these past years, especially in 1968, is the increasing complexity of the issues they are being asked to face. It has been rightly said of World War II that it possessed the two qualities essential to any conflict that makes any sense : goals and moments of laughter. Neither Vietnam nor the racial situation nor the generation gap had presented either a clearly defined objective or a glimmer of humour. In 1968, Richard Nixon was running strong because he is a skilled hand at reducing problems to their simplest elements—in other words, at reaching his audience at their level without committing himself to dangerous specifics.

The Republicans emerged from Miami leaving everyone baffled as to what precisely they had accomplished or agreed on but, most important, giving an impression of internal drive, purpose and confidence. They looked as if they knew where they were going, even if no one else did. In the light of the events in Chicago two weeks later, this was a considerable achievement.

During the festivities in Miami, the Republicans' peace of mind had been hardly scratched by the outbreak of a minor race riot on the outskirts of the city. Out of sight, out of mind, and, as the city authorities hastened to remind everyone, in the event of serious trouble it was always possible to isolate Miami Beach by closing the causeway linking it to the city proper.

Between August 26th and August 30th, there must have been many Democrats who fervently wished that their convention in Chicago could be thus easily immunised by the forces of dis-content. Whatever transpired in the Amphitheatre during those days, it was never for an instant possible to forget that in order to choose their Presidential nominee, delegates and candidates had to be installed behind a barbed-wire stockade protected by the tightest security precautions in political history. Chicago during the convention presented a spectacle in some ways even more frightening than a ghetto during a riot. And yet it seemed altogether a fitting setting for the political decision-making that the Democrats had gathered to achieve.

On the eve of the Democratic convention, Hubert Horatio Humphrey appeared to have as tight a grip on his party's nomination as had Richard Nixon over the Republicans. But this with two vitally important differences: first, Humphrey's strength was plainly derived from the Democratic establishment —the party bosses whom Eugene McCarthy's staggering cam-paign had supposedly done so much to humble. At a time when the Democratic rank and file seemed as desperate as the nation as a whole for change for some kind, the men on whom Humphrey depended seemed to epitomise everything that the dissenters hoped to sweep away. Most of all, it was clear that Humphrey stood on the brink of nomination more than any-thing because of the power and influence of Lyndon Johnson, whom he had refused to disclaim. To the Democratic delegates, whether openly or secretly, President Johnson was the millstone they felt a frantic urge to rid themselves of. All this was closely linked to the second difference between the situation of Humphrey and Nixon: in Nixon's case, it was generally agreed that it was first-class organising and boundless energy that had brought him a return to politics which one commentator called "as remarkable as the raising of Lazarus from the dead". But in Humphrey's case, it had been clear since early April that he was being served by a second-rate staff running a third-rate race. That he had arrived at the post at all was probably thanks as much as anything to the fact that he had been involved in no head-on primary clashes. In that event, he would almost certainly have been crushed long before August 26th. No, Humphrey had not got where he was on his ability as a fighter, nor because of any public mandate. He had merely picked up the pieces—very sizeable pieces—that accrued to a man running on the Administration's coat-tails against no really credible opposition. . . .

No really credible opposition . . . This was one of the remarkable paradoxes of the Democratic Party at the start of its convention. There was within the ranks of the delegates a frantic longing for a new face which prompted many to hope desperately that Senator Edward Kennedy would come forward. Kennedy, who could probably have beaten Richard Nixon without leaving home at Hyannis Port, would not make himself available. He was almost certainly right. The only way in which he could have received the nomination with grace would have been if it had been offered to him, signed, sealed and delivered. What would probably have been disastrous, as he well knew, was if he had come out to fight for it. His aides and friends were measuring his prospects hourly during convention week and, in the end, it was adjudged to be too close for safety. To have fought and lost would have the supreme indignity, given his situation set above the flow of ordinary politics by the family tragedies.

It was, however, a measure of feeling at the convention that a Humphrey aide told me he was certain that, was Robert Kennedy alive and present, he could have beaten Humphrey out of the ground. The delegates were of a mood for an alternative: with all the force and energy and organisation of the Kennedy team, it is more than conceivable that he might have done it, despite the numerical odds against him.

But in all this, alive, offering himself as a candidate, the hero of 1968, Senator Eugene McCarthy should surely be the convention's man. He represented the very soul of change, the

living embodiment of the "new politics". And yet, the Democratic convention overwhelmingly rejected him, and passed a
platform plank on the Vietnam war that seemed to negate all
that he had fought to achieve. Where was McCarthy on August
26th, and how was it possible for him to have failed so badly
where others felt that Robert Kennedy might have succeeded?

The course of the convention witnessed an astonishing turn
around in commentators' attitudes to McCarthy—a continuous
process of critical analysis of both the man and his methods.
Where he had spent the spring and early summer as the focal
point of admiration and wonderment, by convention time it
was being seriously suggested that, with anyone but McCarthy
at their head, the peace campaigners would have had the nomination wrapped up. It's depressing to say that the critics produced
some convincing evidence to support their case.

Eugene McCarthy began the campaign of 1968 as a "loner",
and worked miracles with the electorate. Where he failed disastrously was in remaining a loner to its bitter end. He failed
to accept that in politics compromises must be made—in his
case, such compromises including using diplomacy on the party
regulars who choose Presidential nominees. Instead, he employed throughout the tactics he had used with such success on
the voters at large, and totally ignored the practical politicians.
He is, in his way, a very arrogant man and, while his supporters
tolerated and even admired his distant aloofness, sometimes even
spitefulness, the party bosses would not. By convention time, he
had successfully alienated even many of those anxious to help
him. Despite his staff and his chauffeur-driven cars and his campaign planes, he remained a one-man road show—fighting
alone, thinking alone, almost beyond advice. It was a path that
might be suited to a new politics once established but, in 1968,
the rules of the game were still being dictated by the tradition-
alists.

Beyond even their personal feelings about his methods, the
regular party politicians were frankly unable to envisage Mc-
Carthy as having the energy or the potential to run a national
administration. And in this again, there was little to contradict
them in McCarthy's public pronouncements. He gave the impression that, if elected President, he would simply appoint a
committee to run the country, and retire to a back-room of the
White House to ponder great thoughts. This was a bad year to

advocate McCarthy's particular brand of less powerful presidency, when the nation cried out for a leader who would show them the way to something—whatever that something might be.

"If there was ever any doubt about this convention going to us, the Russians have settled the issue," one Humphrey-man told me on opening day. And it was certainly true that if one more knife was required to doom McCarthy's candidacy, the invasion of Czechoslovakia provided it. It was the final stroke guaranteed to make the convention even less inclined to listen to McCarthy's especial brand of sweet talk. In those last days before the voting, everything seemed to have aligned against the liberals: the last-ditch efforts of Senator George McGovern of South Dakota to rally around him as a candidate those left-wingers unwilling to support McCarthy were plainly fore-doomed. Within hours of arrival in Chicago, it was easy to see that Mayor Richard Daley and his friends planned to control operations both within and without the convention hall in the tightest possible grip, and the demonstrators gathering around the city were obviously likely to push at least a few wavering delegates out of the liberal ranks.

Perhaps the most hopeful developments of either national convention took place even before the opening of the Democrats', at the meetings of their credentials committee debating which delegates should be allowed to take their seats. In the space of a week, the committee heard delegations from a string of Southern states charged with racism in the selection of their members. Hour after hour, integrated delegations demanded to be seated in place of the official and segregated ones, and brought forth case after case of petty corruption and wretched abuse of party processes. When the hearings were over, the entire official Mississippi delegation was unseated, and the Georgia official delegates were forced to accept a slate of rival delegates to make up half their voting power. It was a stinging lesson for the South, and a remarkable show of determination by the committee and its chairman, Governor Richard Hughes of New Jersey. The committee's action required considerable nerve, because at a time when every Democrat was aware of the danger of losing the November election, it was clear that to unseat Southern delegates would upset many potential supporters back home. The credentials committee's decision represented perhaps the only triumph of principle over practical politics at either convention.

On Monday night, the first session of the convention, a drama was enacted a few miles from the Amphitheatre in Chicago's Lincoln Park that was in its way as important as proceedings within the hall. For months before, hippies, protestors and demonstrators of every shade and colour had been threatening that, come convention time, hell would break loose in the city. They promised that hundreds of thousands of young militants would come to Chicago to express their feelings about Lyndon Johnson, the Vietnam war and the Democrats in general. In the event there can at no time have been more than 6,000 to 7,000 protestors active during the convention. But to face them, Mayor Richard Daley had arrayed a show of force that would have bothered a Vietcong army. Daley is tough, and proud of it. He has run Chicago for thirteen years by taking no nonsense from anyone, especially the black minority, and by making a virtue of political corruption on the grounds that he likes power for power's sake, not for personal financial reward. He is an anachronism—the last of the great city bosses, in a tradition that goes straight back to the days of Al Capone and before. But his power in Chicago is absolute and, at the last city election, he collected seventy-three per cent of the vote. He is an important part of America in 1968, because there is no question that the white lower middle class both in his city and across the nation respect his attitudes and even love him for them. He bought the Democratic convention for Chicago at a price of around a million dollars—standard political practice—and he was determined to keep it, to run it and to see that everything was done his way. When the hippy invasion demanded to sleep in the city's Lincoln Park, which normally has an 11 p.m. curfew, he refused their request. On the nights before the convention opening, the police had already ejected numbers of those attempting to bed down. Now, on Monday night, both hippies and police decided to make a night of it.

Soon after 11 p.m., the protestors, chanting "We want our park!" and "Stay! Stay! Stay!" formed a barricade along one ridge, lined it 3,000 strong, and waited to see what the police were going to do about it. They waited for upwards of an hour, beating their drums and yelling and catcalling—daring the law to take them out. Now, while their actions may have been provocative, it is presumably the aim of the law to keep its head while everyone else is losing theirs. Left to themselves, the hippies, who were attacking no one and nothing, would have got bored, tired or indifferent. The police, however, could not spare the time. Deploying like Roman legionaries in massive lines several hundred strong, with their baby-blue riot helmets and carbines and night-sticks, they advanced out of the darkness, hurling tear-gas as they came. The hippies, driven headlong in retreat, reached the other side of the park, choking and retching and outraged. A pitched battle ensued on the streets around the park, during which the police attacked anything that moved: newsmen, cameramen, spectators, hippies—hurling them to the ground, lashing them with their night-sticks, driving them in herds hither and thither. By night's end, only one thing had been accomplished: everyone was good and mad.

It was a pattern that continued throughout the week. It is unnecessary to recap on details of each occurrence, save to say that by Thursday machine guns, armoured personnel carriers, gas grenade launchers, 5,600 fully armed troops and jeeps with barbed-wire cowcatchers on the front had all been brought into action. At one awful moment, when 5,000 demonstrators were massed, standing and singing outside the Hilton Hotel in the centre of downtown, a wedge of police without warning or provocation smashed straight into their centre. They pinned several hundreds—again including newsmen and spectators—against the wall of the Hilton, and for fifteen minutes hammered and hammered and hammered at every living thing in sight. It was a terrifying spectacle—a kind of prisoner-of-war column of terrified young men and girls cringing past a line of police, hands on their heads or in the air, still being kicked to the ground and beaten at every opportunity. Perhaps this was indeed the climax, in that it was the most outrageous incident witnessed by the most disinterested observers—but it was only a part of a pattern. For a reporter, nightly tear-gassing became part of the job. Troops with fixed bayonets became part of the scenery both inside and outside the Hilton headquarters hotel. And casualties and unbelievable comments from the police became a way of life.

Much of this was seen by America on its TV screens. It did very much to damage the Democrats, but it did more to frighten the reasonable-minded: in a poll taken a few days after the convention, seventy-one per cent of Americans said that they thought Mayor Daley had done the right thing. And let it be clear that Mayor Daley's orders and Mayor Daley's support were with the police from beginning to end. A hard core of the demonstrators in Chicago that week were there because they cared desperately about issues and wanted their voices heard. A very small minority indeed came actively hoping to stir up trouble. But the great majority were carefree, gay and, yes, silly young curiosity-seekers. During that week, I saw only a handful of unprovoked incidents caused by the demonstrators. The vast majority of bottles hurled and battles joined came only in retaliation for obvious police brutality. Of course the demonstrators were irresponsible, of course they were childish. But Richard Daley created a miniature police state in Chicago for convention week, to protect the city from . . . nothing. It was afterwards suggested (by Hubert Humphrey, among others) that lives and property were in danger. But for Daley's orders and actions, the demonstrations threatened no one and nothing except the flow of traffic along the city's Michigan Avenue.

The depressing aspect of the situation was that so many Americans approved of Daley's doings: I think that their attitude may be much like that of Chicago policemen I spoke to during the disturbances. They were frightened by the hippies and the yippies and the long-haired protestors—because they didn't understand them. Black Nationalists they feel they can cope with: "They shoot at us, we shoot at them. . . ." But a young girl in jeans who walks along the ranks of National Guardsmen after one holocaust offering them chewing gum and cigarettes? They are bothered. In their terms, it does not add up.

For the Democrats, however, it added up all too painfully. By Thursday night, when Hubert Humphrey made an acceptance speech stressing "law and order" in a way that might have made Richard Nixon jealous, it was clear that much of the blood of Chicago must rub off on the Democrats' prospects in November. In the hall itself, abuse was being thrown at Daley and the Illinois delegation because of events downtown which brought Daley scowling to his feet, shaking his fist in a manner Caligula would have envied. The mask finally dropped that Thursday night when, to ensure himself an ovation from the hall, Daley unashamedly packed the galleries with his own wardsmen, bringing them through the tightest security checks with questionably-procured tickets, to yell "We love Daley" for him. No one was fooled. It was the final proof of the man's obsolescence, to employ a gambit that was old when American politics were still young.

Hubert Humphrey on the night of his acceptance speech seemed to many of those present to have won the most meaningless nomination conceivable.

Senator Eugene McCarthy had announced that he would not support him, and many of McCarthy's young followers were expected to abstain also. The taste of a "rigged" convention was strong in the air and rancour still bristled among the forty per cent or so of the delegates who had fought unsuccessfully to get a liberal Vietnam plank written into the party platform. Beside Humphrey stood Senator Muskie from Maine, his Vice-Presidential nominee, a man far more convincing than but as little known as Richard Nixon's Spiro Agnew, of whom the joke was already made: "Spiro who?"

Downtown, television viewers could see the solid wall of troops that encircled the Hilton Hotel. Several hundreds arrested, dozens injured, lurid photographs in every newspaper in the land, delegates and TV reporters beaten up on the floor of the convention, galleries publicly known to have been packed: this was the background for Humphrey's victorious acceptance speech. Wherever he had gone in Chicago, the Vice-President had met as many boos as cheers. A cartoonist depicted Lyndon Johnson, despite his absence from the convention, as the puppeteer moving his dummies from above the stage. Russell Baker of the *New York Times* likened the conventioneers' feeling to those of men attending their first hanging—with the uneasy feeling that it was their own.

Humphrey had shown quickly before, during and after the convention how he planned to run his race: he was putting all his trust in old-style politics, old-style rhetoric, old-style personalities, and to hell with everything that had happened since the New Hampshire primary.

It is no exaggeration to say that the two party nominating conventions plunged the country into a gloom as deep as any in 1968. No one could say with certainty what was wanted, only what was not. "Not" included, without a shadow of doubt, both Richard Nixon and Hubert Humphrey, a choice the devil himself would not care to have to make. As the year went on, Humphrey's public pronouncements had become almost indistinguishable from those of Nixon. The only difference was that Nixon sounded the more self-assured. "Law and order" had become the central election issue, with each candidate vying to be tougher than the other in his promises of restoring peace. Someone—I think it was Mayor Lindsay—remarked unhappily that one could not have order without justice. And it was certainly true that the popular interpretation of the phrase "law and order" encompassed only the wholly negative aspects: tougher courts, more police, and a close watch on Supreme Court decisions in case they got too liberal.

Before the Democratic convention, it had been possible for many people to argue that Hubert Humphrey was preferable to Nixon because he seemed at heart a profoundly decent man. His ruthless attitude to Mayor Daley's handling of the demonstrators somewhat changed all that. It began to be recalled again that, while Humphrey indeed had a liberal past in the 1940s and 1950s, there was little doubt that his support for the Vietnam war had come from more than loyalty to the President —also from his heart. In the days following the convention, more and more liberal voices announced either that they planned not to vote at all, or that they planned to support, strangely enough, Richard Nixon. A feeling had arisen that at least Nixon was flying under his true colours, and those of his party. It had become questionable whether this could be said of Hubert Humphrey. The two political conventions had proved nothing save that the party regulars could still exert amazing degrees of control in the face of rebellion, and that the Republicans' search for party unity had proved infinitely more successful than that of the Democrats. Nelson Rockefeller announced his support for erstwhile rival Nixon after the convention, whereas in 1964 he had declined to bow gracefully to Barry Goldwater. The Democrats, who had seemed as splintered as they could get before Chicago, emerged having battered themselves almost to death in front of the nation. The demonstrators had at least partly achieved their published goals, to "expose the machinery of repression and the hypocrisy of democracy and free speech", and to help prove that the Democratic nomination had nothing to do with popular support. It was argued after Chicago that at least the debate that had taken place there had been conducted at a more serious level than that among the Republicans. If this was the case, precious little seemed to emerge from it. The lull between the Kennedy assassination and Miami had half-way convinced one that America, after all, was not nearly as frightening a place as one had come to believe. By week's end in Chicago, one lay awake in bed thinking about marching troops and billy-clubbing police. Throughout the convention, I had seriously regretted not taking seriously all the jokes beforehand about coming equipped with flak-jacket, helmet, and gas mask.

On September 2nd, 1968, the following letter appeared in the correspondence column of the New York Times:

To the Editor:

The cynical and degrading business in Chicago constitutes a cruel abuse of our democratic institutions. The war-lovers will doubtless remind us that we have no choice but to vote for the Democratic Party's nominee unless we want to see Richard Nixon in the White House.

It must be insisted that this problem is wholly theirs, all the more so now that the Chicago police and plainclothesmen will be turning to other work.

For anyone who takes his vote seriously as a matter of conviction, the tactical subtleties of conventional politics will exercise no attraction in this tragic year.

I, for one, will not vote for the Democratic nominee, although I have been a registered Democrat for twenty-four years. Abstaining in November I urge other Democrats to do the same.

I accept the risk in utter revulsion. It seems to me that an electorate which could conceivably go for Hubert Humphrey deserves to end up with Richard Nixon.

Charles C. Adler Jnr.,
Associate Professor of History,
Hamilton College,
Clinton, N.Y.

CHAPTER 9

HOW TO STOP WORRYING AND LEARN TO LOVE MAIN STREET

"I'm covering the roof with a high-powered rifle and my best friend's in the elevator shaft."
> Chicago policeman in the Hilton Hotel,
> Democratic convention, August, 1968

R<small>EMEMBERING BACK</small>, T<small>O</small> New Hampshire and to Chicago and to Bobby Kennedy and to Memphis, how impossible it seemed that America in November could present a picture so little different from that in January. One must immediately qualify that, of course, by adding that some things could never be the same again: too many dead, too many hurt in mind as well as body, too much overturned. But from a political standpoint, the withdrawal of Lyndon Johnson seemed at the time to signal the end of something. And yet, what real difference between was being offered Hubert Humphrey in November and Lyndon Johnson in March? Not enough, the American electorate decided. It's said that the Presidency reduces big men and blows up small men to reach about the right size in office. Has Richard Nixon got the stuff of greatness? It's hard to believe.

I am in no sense an expert on America, indeed, before August, 1967, I knew very little indeed about the country. Even now, almost everything I do know is based simply on what I've seen and heard in the space of more than a year there. It can be argued that I have absorbed a false and crooked picture, if only because so much of my time there was spent in covering the nation's tragedies and horrors rather than its many triumphs and victories. The best foreign correspondents can observe without rancour and I don't pass this test because, many times in 1968, I found myself bitter, upset and angry. And these, of course, are to some extent the vices of being young. I have met few people in recent months who were capable of agreeing for more than five minutes on any aspect of America's situation in 1968. I have been knocked down more times than I care to remember for making criticisms of American society which simply cannot withstand close analysis. For this reason, I only hope that I have succeeded in reporting enough facts, enough events, enough personalities in these pages to enable anyone who wishes to ignore my own comments and make his own.

I think it's very important to consider that, looking at America's problems, one must be struck by how many of them are obviously those which stem not from some flaw in the American character, but simply from the United States being the most highly-developed country in the world. The nation's position in this regard has raised a multitude of issues which she is being called on to face, not alone, merely first. So much of the criticism heaped upon America's failings relate to her failure to make good use of her enormous surplus wealth. Such criticisms only seem valid if one recalls that no other society has yet been in a position to have to face this problem, nor to see whether human reaction is any different anywhere else.

In 1968, dimensions and great issues changed course almost before anyone had had time to consider them. For example, until July of this year, it could be argued with some conviction that most Black Nationalists only delivered their rhetoric on the ideal of armed rebellion to frighten the white middle classes. But then came the battle in Cleveland, during which black militant Ahmed Evans, with a group of followers, all heavily armed, engaged in deliberate pitched battle with the forces of the law. Was this an isolated case, or a sign of things to come? Whichever, it is food for more thought. It is being suggested that the days of massive city riots on the scale of Watts or Detroit are over, that guerilla warfare and a reign of terror against the police will now be the tactics of the ghetto. But this again is a question no one would care to attempt to answer definitively.

In the wake of the student riot at Columbia and the demonstrations at the Democratic convention, young white student leaders, more disenchanted than ever by the demise of Eugene McCarthy, are talking of taking their battles too to the streets. If this comes to pass, will there be an escalation on the part of the authorities to match Mayor Daley's actions in Chicago? And most complex of all, even with Richard Nixon in the

White House, how long will the Vietnam war drag on, sapping the innermost fibre of America, and dividing the nation deeper and deeper?

In the later months of 1968, I was astonished by the vehemence of political discussion across the country, even at a dinner-party level. Tempers frayed and friendships bent in the constant ding-dong argument that seemed inescapable at any social get-together. Liberals, rent in their own ranks, nevertheless clustered closer together for mutual security in the face of the increasing conservative tide that crossed the country, and to which both Presidential candidates bowed in their campaigns.

There came to be something almost pathetic about the Presidential campaigns of both Nixon and Humphrey. It somehow seemed absurd that any reasonable man should *want* to take over the nation at this moment in its history. The quest for power and the energy bound up in the election race seemed almost as irrelevant as had proceedings in the Democratic convention hall at a moment when, a few miles away, police were smashing their way through a sea of human flesh.

During 1968, a feeling which began among news gatherers early in the year gradually spread through the whole of America : it was one of constant apprehensive anticipation. Reporters reached the point where, as soon as returned from covering a riot or an assassination, they began to wonder how soon the next would take place. This spread until almost everyone came to accept the idea that the crisis had not ended, would not end tomorrow, and would in any case be replaced by a new one the day after.

"I think," someone said to me matter-of-factly at a New York cocktail party, "that it's going to be about the fourth assassination that will bring everyone to their senses." He was entirely serious. Like everyone else, without tangible reason, he expected it. This seems no way to enjoy living. But then, nor is it entertaining to know that one's statistical chances of being murdered, raped, robbed or otherwise attacked are rather too high to be funny. I found during my stay in the US that it was possible to enjoy New York, San Francisco, certain people, certain places. But it was never possible to enjoy America in the way that one can Greece or Italy or other countries, in the broader and general sense.

The ultimate victory of Richard Nixon on November 5th was far less surprising for the fact than for Hubert Humphrey's dramatic come-back in the last days of October. Could it be, when the chips were down, that many Americans simply awoke to a feeling of revulsion at the idea of supporting in Nixon the last great political hack?

Having run his race to the Republican Convention with flawless precision, Nixon had then made one bad mistake and taken another sizeable gamble. His mistake was the choice of Spiro Agnew as his Vice-Presidential candidate, despite the immediate political advantage he gained at the Convention by bowing to Southern preferences in this direction. Agnew, during the eight weeks before the election, acquired a reputation for dropping bricks which Hubert Humphrey might have envied. Nor were his mistakes very amusing ones: in the rush to prove himself more conservative than his conservative leader, Agnew hurled charges of communism with the abandon of a Joseph McCarthy. His performance became all the more pathetic when contrasted with that of Humphrey's running-mate, Edmund Muskie, the one dynamic new face to be thrown up by the last stages of the election. Between the Convention and polling day, Agnew's gaffes probably cost Nixon as many votes as Lyndon Johnson's last moment decision to halt the bombing of North Vietnam.

Nixon's great gamble, in the run-up to the election, was his decision that it was safer to say nothing at all in his public pronouncements and be accused of being trickily reticent than to make firm statements which might alienate sectors of the electorate whom he already had behind him. The Nixon strategy was based on the negative assumption that he had as good as won the election if he could only avoid some active disaster. It was a policy that brought him within a hair's-breadth of defeat.

For Hubert Humphrey, working his via dolorosa from the wreckage of the Democratic Convention, the path could only have been uphill. But even for those alienated by his performance at the Convention, there had to be a wisp of sympathy for Humphrey's fate at the hands of Lyndon Johnson. The President, wounded, chastened and furiously angry, appeared bent on embarrassing every move of Humphrey's towards the White House. He contradicted his Vice-President several times when the latter made faintly liberal statements on Vietnam. He waited until too late to take the steps towards peace in Vietnam himself which, a mere week earlier, might have saved the Humphrey cause. Eugene McCarthy, too, gave his grudging endorsement to Hubert's candidacy too late to affect the outcome. McCarthyites had many of them been far too deeply wounded to return thus easily to the fold.

America went to the polls in a mood of deep depression, faced with a choice between two men almost equally lacklustre. The only candidate who really aroused the enthusiasm of his followers was George Wallace, whose influence, mercifully, was less great in the outcome than had been feared. But nine million Americans were sufficiently fraught, full of hate, full of confusion, to cast their votes for him. And it is arguable that he lost the Southern states for Humphrey, who might otherwise have had that shade of the odds that would have enabled him to win.

And above, or perhaps beneath it all, Lyndon Johnson: as 1968 drew to its close, he might count himself with Martin Luther King and Robert Kennedy—a desperate casualty of a fatal year. When he announced his withdrawal in March, he had seen it as the supreme gesture of statesmanship that would assure him his place in history. Now, with a new shadow waiting impatiently to climb the steps of the White House, all his dreams were left in ruins. Peace in Vietnam had proved a desperately elusive goal, his personal popularity remained negligible, and the Congress in his declining months had missed no opportunity to slight him unmercifully. Justice of the Supreme Court Abe Fortas had withdrawn his own name as Chief Justice, after Johnson's nomination of him had been humiliatingly beaten about in the Senate. Nor could the President leave office much loved by his own Party: his treatment of Hubert Humphrey during the latter's campaign had taken care of that.

The spectre of a deadlocked election had made even polling day itself a nightmare. As little as a week before, Nixon seemed assured of a runaway victory, borne home by the tide of conservatism across the country. But his own fumbling and the desperate last-minute efforts of the Democratic camp brought Humphrey almost level, presenting a threat that the election might have to be decided in the Congress if neither man got a clear majority. But it is fair to say that even Humphrey's late run represented no triumph for liberalism : the Wallace forces which brought the situation about were those of the right, not the left.

It's difficult to believe that these next four years will be good ones in which to live in America. Put crudely, the mandate of Richard Nixon is, for practical purposes, one of domestic repression. This was an election carried by the "un-black, the un-young, the un-poor", and it is these people who have put Nixon in office to . . . get them peace and quiet at any price. To this end, they expect tougher courts, tougher police, less welfare assistance to the under-privileged, and no more Vietnams. In Washington, there will be an overturn in government personnel of a kind unseen since 1960. It is sad to say that Richard Nixon has always seemed an attractive figure compared with some of the men he gathers around him.

The most alarming aspect of the situation is the widening of the gulf that can be expected between the forces of liberalism, the young, and the black, and those of the establishment. The death of Robert Kennedy had already left a sad void among major politicians capable of communicating with the under-privileged. The election of Richard Nixon will complete the process. For the Southern Negro, the prospect of change and reform has receded even more than for those in the North. George Wallace's showing in the Southern states at the election has broadened his power base, and it is highly unlikely that Nixon will be prepared to take forceful action towards racial progress in the South. He enters office with the political weakness of a man who has only won election by a whisker, and is all the less able to take decisive actions because of this.

It is difficult to believe that Hubert Humphrey can remain in the forefront of the Democratic Party. He falls with the old regime, and leaves as his legacy only Muskie, his former running-mate. Many observers are already suggesting that in 1972 it will be Edmund Muskie and Edward Kennedy who will be competing for the Party leadership. Eugene McCarthy? Who knows what goes on in that complicated academic mind. For him, 1968 has been the magnificent hour. He rose from relative obscurity to the status of national crusader, and was defeated by a coalition of such unpleasant forces that it was no shame for him. Whether he has the will or the ability to remain in the political forefront, however, must depend heavily on the course of the next four years. Also, perhaps, on whether he is prepared to widen the base of his support to include the urban Negro, whom he almost ignored for much of his 1968 campaign. Without the urban Negro, his position in practical politics must remain questionable. But if he could forge a new liberal alliance, rallying together all the disenchanted forces, he might have another chance to shatter the political establishment. Come what may, however, his place among the phenomena of modern American politics has been assured. To him goes the honour of having accomplished the impossible for the first, if not the last time in 1968.

Poor America. Never has there been a time when she seemed so badly to need things to go right, and never have they gone so disastrously wrong as in 1968. Pessimists have suggested that a comparison may emerge between the United States under a Nixon Administration and Germany in the days of the Weimar Republic. This seems to place too little faith in America's astonishing capacity for resilience. But the Russians did more than even they knew when they invaded Czechoslovakia, for they frightened many Americans badly. In the same way, it is difficult to see the course for Black Nationalism within the United States, when it seems certain that if there is more militance, there will be more white conservatism, and if there is no militance, there will be renewed white apathy.

This is no place, however, to make more speculative comments or attempt rash judgements. What is the most significant, if unhappy way to remember America in 1968? Perhaps it is enough to say that when I left Chicago after the Democratic National Convention, I suddenly found that I had stopped noticing the National Guardsmen who were walking into the coffee shop of the Hilton Hotel with their rifles still slung over their shoulders.

And now Nixon is President . . .

SELECT BIBLIOGRAPHY

SELECT BIBLIOGRAPHY

While by no means any kind of comprehensive list, these are a few of the books I found most helpful in understanding America in 1968:

Clark, Kenneth B. *Dark Ghetto: Dilemmas of Social Power.* New York: Harper & Row, 1965.

Cleaver, Eldridge. *Soul on Ice.* New York: McGraw-Hill, 1968.

Fortas, Abe. *Concerning Dissent and Civil Disobedience.* Cleveland: World Publishing Company, 1968.

Kennedy, Robert F. *To Seek a Newer World.* New York: Doubleday & Co., 1968.

The Autobiography of Malcolm X. New York: Grove Press, 1965.

Packard, Vance. *The Status Seekers.* New York: David McKay Co., 1959.

Report of the National Advisory Commission on Civil Disorders. New York: Bantam, 1968.

Schlesinger, Arthur. *A Thousand Days: John F. Kennedy in the White House.* Boston: Houghton Mifflin, 1965.

Sherrill, Robert, and Ernst, Harry. *HHH The Drugstore Liberal: Hubert Humphrey in Politics.* New York: Grossman Publishers, 1968.

White, Theodore. *The Making of the President 1960.* New York: Atheneum Publishers, 1960.

———. *The Making of the President 1964.* New York: Atheneum Publishers, 1964.

INDEX

INDEX

ABC network, 141
Abernathy, Rev. Ralph, 60, 63, 77–81
Adler, Charles C., his letter to *New York Times*, 169
Advertisers, their influence on television programmes, 142–3, 145
Agnew, Spiro, 156, 158, 166, 174
Alabama, 48
Alcohol consumption, 126
Allen, Ivan (Mayor of Alberta), 66–9
Appalachia, 80
Arkansas, 134
Arms. *See* Firearms
Associated Press, 140
Association of Commerce and Industry, 45
Atlanta (Georgia), 62–3, 65–70, 77, 146
Atlanta Constitution, 68

Baker, Russell, 166
Bell, Daniel, on the values of the middle class, 118
Black Nationalism, 46–51, 165, 172, 177
Breslin, Jimmy, 149
Broadcasting. *See* Radio; Television
Brooke, Senator Edward, 51
Brown, Rap, 45
Buchwald, Art, 140, 146
Buckley, William, 13
Bunche, Ralph, 50

California, 20, 95; University of, 89; primary in, 102
Capone, Al, 163
Carmichael, Stokeley, 31, 45, 46–7
Carter, Hodding, 71

CBS network, 141–4
Censorship, television, 145
Census Bureau, 44
Chicago, 58, 123, 171, 174; racial riots in, 34, 35–9; Jobs Now organization, 44–5; discrimination against Negroes in, 117; Democratic convention held in, 151, 159–63, 165–8; police behaviour against hippies, 163–5, 172
Chicago Tribune, 140
"Children's Crusade, The", 24, 102
China, 132
Cities: middle class migration from centres of, 41–2; financial straits in, 42; arms race in, 123–4; opposition to Federal tax for development, 127; attempts to improve the lot of Negroes in, 127; Open Housing issue, 127–8; urban planning in New York, 130–1
Civil disobedience issue, 86–7
Civil disorders. *See* Riots
Civil Rights movement, 61–6, 70, 72, 74, 77, 81, 127
Civil War, 61, 65
Clark, Ramsay (Attorney-General), 60
Cleage, Rev. Albert, 47–9, 51, 53
Cleveland (Ohio), 151, 172
Columbia University, student disturbances at, 85–6, 172
Commercial Appeal, Memphis, 57
Commission on Civil Disorders, 121; their Report (Riot Report), 51–3, 63, 67, 149
Communism, Communists, 25, 69, 83, 129, 132
Concord (New Hampshire), 24, 27

Congress, 31, 42, 78, 115, 122, 131, 139, 151, 175; appropriations for War on Poverty, 43, 44, 121; and the Poor People's March, 81; Open Housing law, 128
Congressional Quarterly, 139
Conventions, 17, 19
  See also Democratic party; Republican party
Cotton gin, invention of, 64
Crime: committed mainly by the under-privileged, 119; volume of involving firearms, 124
  See also Riots
Cronkite, Walter, 144
Czechoslovakia, 162, 177

Daley, Richard (Mayor of Chicago), 37, 162, 163, 165–6, 167, 172
Daughters of the Confederacy, 63
Day, J. Edward, 21
Delegates: battle for control of, at national conventions, 17; choice of, for national conventions, 18; battle for control of, at primaries, 20
Delta, the. *See* Mississippi Delta
Democratic party, 157, 176; convention at Chicago, 151, 153, 159–63, 165–8, 174
Detroit (Michigan), 51, 58, 64, 147–8; riots in, 13, 39, 172; United Church of Christ, 47
Domestic service, 126
Dow Chemical Corporation, 85
Drug takers, 97

Education Network, 142
Eisenhower, Dwight D., 62
Evans, Ahmed, 151, 172

Federal Communications Commission, 72, 140
Federal troops, 37n.
Firearms, 13; the arms race in the cities, 123–4; volume of crime involving firearms, 124, 125;

Firearms—*continued*
  opposition to gun control, 124–6, 133–4
Fiscal system, effects of, 41–2
  See also Taxation
Food Stamp programme, 42, 43
Ford Foundation, 44, 142
Foreign Relations Committee. *See* Senate
Fortas, Abe, 86, 122, 175
Freedom City (Mississippi), 74
"Freedom Ride" demonstration, 62
Fulbright, Senator William, 104

Gavin, General James, 104
Georgia, 48, 58
Germany, 176–7
Ghettoes, 13, 40–2, 44–5, 47, 49, 52–3, 58, 70, 80, 86, 110–11, 119, 127, 128, 130, 148, 151
Goldwater, Barry, 156, 167; on liberals, 121–2
Goodwin, Richard, 25, 110
Graduate, The (film), 91
Great Society programmes, 42–4
Groppi, Father Jame, 127
Group journalism concept, 147
Guevara, Che, 92

Haley, Alex, 50, 51
Harlem, 86, 151
Head Start scheme, 43
Heller, Walter, 44
Henderson, Vivian, "The Economic Status of Negroes in the Nation and the South", 66n.
Hilton Hotel, Chicago, 164, 166, 174
Hippies, 95–7; in Chicago, 163–5
Hollywood, 96, 110n., 131
House of Representatives. *See* Representatives
Housing: Open Housing issue, 31, 127–8; in New York, 131
Housing and Urban Development Department, 42
Houston (Texas), 125

Hughes, Richard (Governor of New Jersey), 162
Humphrey, Hubert, 13–14, 19, 31, 33, 99, 101, 102, 109, 111, 133, 169, 171, 173; doubts about his policies, 151, 165, 167; lack of ability, and served by poor staff, 159–60; approves Mayor Daley's action, 165, 167; acceptance speech, 165; contradicted by Johnson, 174–5
Huntley-Brinkley, 144

Ignorance, 129
Indiana, 20; primary in, 34, 102, 109, 110
Indians, 79
Institute for Defence Analyses, 86n.
Integration issue, 49–50, 66, 69, 75
Isolationism, 132

Jackson, Jesse, 60
Jackson (Mississippi), 57, 62, 72, 75
Jenkins, Herbert (police chief of Atlanta), 67–8
Jews, 119
Job Corps organization, 43
John Birch Society, 122
Johnson, Lyndon B., 14, 15, 21, 22, 26, 28, 30, 101, 102, 104–7, 109, 122, 151, 157, 159, 163, 166; unpopularity, 22–3, 24; sincerity, 23; and the Wisconsin primary, 29; withdraws from presidential election, 31–2, 33, 171; and the Commission on Civil Disorders, 51; halts bombing in N. Vietnam, 174; contradicts Humphrey, 174–5
Journalism schools, 91

Karenga, Maulana Ron, 48–9, 51, 53
Kefauver, Estes, 25
Kempton, Murray, 22, 113
Kennedy, Senator Edward, 160, 176
Kennedy, Ethel, 107, 109

Kennedy, John F., 19, 21, 25–6, 58, 146
Kennedy, Robert F., 14, 19, 20, 33, 34, 60, 62, 99, 102, 114, 121, 124, 131, 134, 144, 146, 149, 151, 160, 161, 171, 175, 176; enters presidential contest, 30; policies, 101; defeated in Oregon primary, 102; victory in California primary, 102–3; relations with Eugene McCarthy, 105; public effect of his campaign, 107–9; victory in Indiana and Nebraska, 110–11; spell exercised by, 111–13
Kentucky, 79
Khe Sanh, 26
King, Mrs. Coretta, 60, 81
King, Martin Luther, 34, 49, 55, 60, 62–4, 68–9, 76–8, 81–2, 124, 128–9, 133, 146, 149, 175; in Memphis, and assassinated, 57–9
Korea, 22
Kraft, Joseph, 140
Ku Klux Klan, 61, 75

Laurel (Mississippi), 75
Liberals, liberalism, 113, 173, 175, 176
Life, 139
Lincoln, Abraham, 14
Lindsay, John (Mayor of New York), 42, 130–1, 151, 156, 167
Little Rock (Arkansas), 62
Loeb, Henry (Mayor of Memphis), 57, 58
Loeb, William, 146
Look, 139
Los Angeles (California), 49, 80, 146, 149; Watts riots, 39, 172; US movement, 48–9
Los Angeles Times, 147
Louisiana, 48

McCalls magazine, 140
McCarthy, Eugene, 19, 20, 34, 83, 94, 99, 112, 132, 133; victory in New Hampshire primary, 23–9;

McCarthy, Eugene—*continued*
and the Wisconsin primary,
29–30, 32, 102–3, 106; policies,
101; wins Oregon primary, 102,
111; style of speaking, 103–4;
opposes Vietnam war, 104–5;
increases his following, 106;
defeated in Indiana and Nebraska, 110–11; student support
for, 111; on American liberalism, 113; his crusading spirit,
113–14; victory in New York
primary, 151; loses Democratic
nomination, 159–61; alienates
party bosses, 161; the blow to
his hopes, 161–2; endorses Humphrey's candidacy, 175; his
magnificent hour, 176
McCarthy, Senator Joseph, 111,
128–9
McGovern, Senator George, 162
McGrory, Mary, 149
Maddox, Lester (Governor of
Georgia), 63, 66–9
Madison. *See* Wisconsin, Univer-
sity of
Malcolm X, 48
Manchester (New Hampshire), 27
Manchester Union, 146
Marshall, Throogood, 50
Mead, Margaret, on change in
the U.S.A., 130
Mechanization, its effects in the
South, 65
Memphis (Tennessee), 34, 55,
57–63, 124, 149, 171
Mercouri, Melina, 145
Mexicans, 79
Mexico, 31, 33
Miami (Florida), Republican con-
vention held in, 151, 153–9, 174
Michigan, University of, 89, 90
Middle-class, migrates out of city
centres, 41–2; values of, 118;
aims, 119
Migrations: of middle-class from
city centres, 41–2; of Negroes
from the South, 65

Miller, Arthur, on the American
dream, 134
Milwaukee (Wisconsin), 128, 145
Minnesota, 19, 104; University of,
89
Minorities, looked down on by
the WASP, 119
Minutemen, 122
Mississippi, 39, 72, 73, 78
Mississippi Delta, 40, 57, 73–6,
79–81
Montgomery (Alabama), 57, 62,
63, 69, 70, 72, 78
Moynihan Report, 40
Muggeridge, Malcolm, on ignor-
ance in the U.S.A., 129, 139
Murders, 125
Muskie, Senator Edmund, 166,
176

Napalm, 85
National Association for the Advancement of Coloured People
(NAACP), 50, 75
National Guard, 37–8, 52, 59, 67,
69, 119, 174
National Rifle Association, 124
NBC network, 141, 144
Nebraska, 20; primary in, 102,
109–10
Negroes, 34, 126, 134, 146, 148;
and the riots, 35–40; social and
economic conditions, 40–1; and
Poverty Programmes, 42–5;
outlook for the young Negro,
45–6; Stokeley Carmichael's
philosophy and appeal, 46–7;
the Rev. Arthur Cleage, 47–8;
the US movement, 48; and
integration, 49–50; rejection of
the "Uncle Toms", 50–1; the
Report of the Commission on
Civil Disorders, 51–3; the gulf
between rich and poor Negroes,
52–3; the ghetto Negro and
American affluence, 53; and
the assassination of Martin
Luther King, 57–61; and the
Civil Rights movement, 61–4;

Negroes—*continued*
and the Poor People's March,
76–82; join student activists, 86;
in universities, 88; opinion poll
on, 115; discrimination against,
in Chicago, 117; looked down
on by the WASP, 119; business
men and better jobs for, 127;
fears of revolt by, 128–9; bleak
prospects for their amelioration,
176
See also South, the
Never on Sunday (film), 145
New Hampshire, 19, 20, 171;
primary in, 15, 22–3, 26–9,
101–3, 105–6, 154–5
New Orleans (Louisiana), 62
New Republic, 139
New York City, 126, 173; the
Negroes in, 40; garbage strike
in, 57; Mayor Lindsay's re-
forms, 130–1; Public Broadcasting Laboratory, 142
New York State, 130; primary in,
151
New York Times, 139, 140, 146, 147,
166; on McCarthy's peace campaign, 113; Professor Adler's
letter to, 169
Newark (New Jersey), 39, 63
Newspapers, 73, 139–40, 146–50
Newsweek, 139, 140, 148–9
Nielsen Audience Survey, 137
Nixon, Richard, 14, 21, 22, 26, 28,
33, 40, 99, 120, 133, 151, 165–7,
169, 171, 173, 176, 177; brilli-
ance of his campaign, 153; hold
on his delegates, 154, 159;
policies, 155; chooses vice-
presidential nominee, 156, 174;
wins Republican nomination,
156–8; organizing ability and
energy, 159–60; wins presidential election, 174, 175; his great
mistake, 174
NRA. *See* National Rifle Association

Office of Economic Opportunity,
43

Omaha (Nebraska), 111, 112
Open Housing issue, 31, 127–8
Oregon, 20, 124; primary in, 102,
111
Overseas Press Club, 107

Packard, Vance, *The Status Seekers*,
123
Periodicals, 139, 140, 148–9
Philadelphia (Pennsylvania), 39,
124
Police: and student revolts, 87;
fear and dislike of, 123; prepara-
tions for disorders, 123–4; be-
haviour in Chicago, 164–5
Poor People's March, 76–82
Poor whites, 64, 65, 79
Poverty, 137; Poverty Pro-
grammes, 42–5
Presidential candidates, their be-
hind-the-scenes activities, 18
Primaries; their purpose, 18,
19–20; not held in all states, 19,
20; finance, 19
Professionalism, 91
Public assistance, 45
Public Broadcasting Laboratory,
New York, 142
Public dissent, rights of, 86

Quotations from Chairman LBJ, 22

Racial discrimination, 41
See also Negroes
Radio, 72, 139
Ray, James, 60*n.*
Reader's Digest, 140
Reagan, Ronald (Governor of
California), 154, 156, 157
Representatives, House of, 26, 115
Republican party, 131, 151, 167;
convention at Miami, 151–9,
174
Resurrection City, 79–81
Riot Commission. *See* Commission
on Civil Disorders
Riots, 14, 83; in Detroit, 13, 39,
172; in Chicago, 34–9, 55; in
Los Angeles, 39, 172; Report of

Riots—*continued*
the Commission on Civil Disorders, 51–3; at Columbia University, 85–6, 172; the dilemma caused by, 119; anti-riot preparations, 123–4; in Miami, 159
Rizzo, Frank (police chief of Philadelphia), 124
Rockefeller, Nelson (Governor of New York), 21, 99, 133, 151, 154, 156–7, 167
Rockefeller, Governor Winthrop, 134
Rockefeller Foundation, 44
Romney, George (Governor of Michigan), 21–2, 151–2
Roosevelt, F. D., 22
Roper Research Survey, 137
Rural communities, 127
Rustin, Bayard, 80

Salinger, Pierre, 31, 33
Salisbury, Harrison, 147
San Francisco (California), 95–7, 126, 148, 173
Schlesinger, Arthur, 30–1
School segregation, 62, 70
Seeger, Pete, 142–3
Segregation, segregationists, 57–8, 61–2, 69–71
Selma (Alabama), 62
Senate Foreign Relations Committee, 104
Sevareid, Eric, 144
Sioux Falls (South Dakota), 15
Slavery, 64–5
Slums, 41, 42
See also Ghettoes
Smith, Stephen, 30
Smothers Brothers Comedy Hour, 142, 145
Social Security Act (1935), 43
Sorensen, Theodore, 30, 107
South, the: Memphis and the Assassination of Martin Luther King, 57–61; the Civil Rights movement, 61–4; economic position of the Negro, 64–6; Atlanta, Georgia, 66–70; George Wall-

South—*continued*
ace, and segregation, 70–2; television and radio, 72–3, 144–5; the Negroes of the Mississippi Delta, 73–6; and the Supreme Court, 122; votes for Wallace in presidential election, 175, 176
South Dakota, 126
Southern Christian Leadership Conference, 77–81
Spock, Benjamin, 104
Status, materialism of, 123
Strickland, Joe, 13
Strikes, 57–8, 148
Student activists, 24, 83; their demands, 85; Columbia University disturbances, 85–6; attitudes and tactics, 86–7; intensity of their revolts, 87; vagueness of aims, 87–8; inevitability of their protest, 92; the hardcore activists small in number, 92–3; reasons for university disagreements, 93–4; and the character of American society, 97–8
See also Universities
Supreme Court. See United States Supreme Court

Taxation, 118, 126
Television, 129, 137, 139, 147, 148; in the South, 72; number of stations, 140; system of control, 140–1; the great networks, 141; finance, 141–2; Education Network, 142; influence of advertisers, 142–3, 145; and the Vietnam war, 143–4; censorship by local stations, 144–5; failure in public service, 145–6, 149; quality of outside broadcasts, 146
Texas, 126
Thurmond, Strom, 156
Time magazine, 103, 132, 139, 140, 148–9; on Kennedy's campaign, 109

Truman, H. S., 22, 25

United Press International, 140
United States Supreme Court, 122-3
Universities: finance, 88; part-time earnings by students, 88-9; the staff, 88-90; as power structures, 90-1; and education for an end, 91; self-confidence of students, 91-2; three alternatives for the student, 94-5; mode of life of hedonistic students, 95-7
See also Student activities
Urban renewal plan, 42
See also Cities
US movement, 48-9

Vietnam, 13, 21, 23-6, 32, 33, 37n., 41, 62, 83, 94, 99, 104, 106, 120, 126-7, 129, 132, 137, 143-4, 146-7, 151, 158, 161, 163, 167, 173, 175; student opposition to the war, 85; Lyndon Johnson halts bombing of the North, 174

Violence. See Firearms; Police; Riots; Student activists
VISTA, 43
Voter registration, in Mississippi, 73

Wall Street Journal, 139, 140, 146, 147
Wallace, George, 26, 40, 64, 65, 69-71, 134, 145, 175, 176

Wallace, Lurleen (Governor of Alabama), 69-71, 78
War on Poverty, 43
Warren, Earl, 123
Washington, George, 17
Washington DC, 13, 15, 28, 42, 89, 176; Dodge House Hotel, 31; Housing and Urban Development Dept., 42; riots in, 55; Poor People's March on, 77-82
Washington Post, 29, 139, 140, 147; on the Commission to consider Violence, 121
WASP (White Anglo-Saxon Protestant American), outlook of, 119-20
Watts riots. See Los Angeles
West Virginia, 20
White, Theodore, 22; The Making of the President, 18, 28-9; on primaries, 20
White House, 27, 28, 139
Wild in the Streets (film), 92
Wilkins, Roy, 50
Williams, Hosea, 60
Wisconsin, 20, 90; primary in, 29-30, 102, 106; University of, 91
World War I, 65
World War II, 127, 158
Write-in vote, 18
Wycoff, Gene, on advertising and television, 143

Young Andrew, 60, 81
Young, Whitney, 46, 50